Strip Down & Wake Up

SELF
REALIZATION
—— FOR ——
REGULAR PEOPLE

NO CHANTING, YOGA PANTS,
OR HARD DRUGS REQUIRED

ANASTASIA NETRI

Strip Down & Wake Up

SELF REALIZATION
FOR REGULAR PEOPLE

NO CHANTING, YOGA PANTS,
OR HARD DRUGS REQUIRED

By: Anastasia Netri

Copyright © 2017 by Anastasia Netri

Legal Disclaimer

The information provided in this book solely and also completely represents the views of the author as of the date of publication. Any minor to, or potential misrepresentation of, any individual or companies is entirely unintentional. As a result of changing information, conditions or contexts, this author reserves the right to alter content or option with impunity. The information in this e-book may be very useful and is sold with the knowledge that neither the author nor publisher is engaged in presenting specific psychological, emotional, or sexual advice. Nor is anything in this book intended to be a diagnosis, prescription, recommendation or cure for any specific kind of psychological, emotional, or sexual problem. Each person has unique needs, and this book cannot take these individual differences into accounts.

Table of Contents

1 Are You Ready to Wake Up?

My self-realization experience, my moment of waking up, was pretty anti-climactic. I wasn't doing Ayahuasca or fresh out of yoga class. It was made up of a lot of years of gradual awakening only to be met with a "Oh. Yeah. Duh!" moment that changed everything and nothing at the same time.

In this book I'll offer insight into the things that are keeping you asleep, suffering, and pushing against your own nature. You are here to self-realize, to wake up, to live a life that is an authentic experience and expression of you. I'll share a few parts of my story that I feel would be useful to your awakening. We will go on a journey together that will bring an array of ahas, realizations, and even some of your own "Oh. Yeah. Duh!" kind of moments.

Am I crazy?

For as long as I can remember, I wondered if I was crazy. I saw the world in a way that no other person was able to validate for me. I tried *so* hard to fit in that I rarely shared with anyone what I was able to see. I had a lot of awareness about things that would be useful to humanity freeing itself and thriving. Even at a young age, I looked at the world like "Wait - why are we doing *this*? There is a smarter way to interact and live!" This wasn't just one thing - it was everything.

From the way I saw people raising children, educating them, the family structure, marriage and relationships, work and careers, the monetary system, pretty much everything that most people think of as "the way it is." Never did any of it make sense to me. I felt like I was living in an insane asylum for most of my life. Couldn't anyone else see what I saw?

So, I repressed, denied, and downright hated who I was. I internalized the labels and projections of others. I had a consistent dilemma: I wanted to fit in, but I hated everything I was trying to fit into because I could see the insanity of it. I kept trying to fix *myself* so I could fit in, be liked, and accepted by others. The suffering and anxiety I went through became so extreme that I often wanted to die to escape from it, from this nightmare.

I became a seeker of self-realization in my 30's. I was seeking not because I wanted to be me, but I wanted to be something that would match up with some image that I thought I was going to finally be: that person who was "lovable," whatever that looked like in my egoic fantasy world. I got on the spiritual path to escape myself, not to embrace it - even though I never would have admitted that to myself at the time. The further I went, the more I understood that there was no escape - I had to face what I was hiding or I would forever be imprisoned by it. I would forever be in the waking nightmare of living a not-enough life. That's when my focus went from "being spiritual" to waking up and experiencing a full self-realization.

The commitment to awakening became the North Star that guided my life. As I became more and more aware, I saw no higher purpose for my life than the course I was on. Nothing else seemed to matter, once I understood that any staying asleep to who I was would forever be one form of overcompensation or another, a life of trying to "get," and a consistent longing for some future salvation that would never come. That wasn't going to work for me.

On the other side of awake

On the other side of it, I can say that finally waking up from my nightmare was nothing like I thought it would be, and everything I thought it would be all at the same time. It was simply a falling away of the false ego (aka feeling "not enough") and what was *trying* to be as a result. That's it. Nothing about me changed. My unique insights, voice, style, and genius were all still there - but without any resistance. It wasn't that I accepted myself - it was deeper than that. The "I" and "myself" were no longer two separate things. There was only "I." Nothing there to try to accept or deny who I was. The false, fantasy image melts, and what is left there is truth.

The way I got to this awareness is unique to me, and doesn't match up with any other story I've heard about the experience itself. I've heard of people having these amazing mystical experiences; mine was quite unextraordinary. No matter how the experience happens or what it is, the result is the same for every other awakened person. After you wake up, there will only be one of you remaining. There will no longer be "parts" of you.

You will not be fragmented. You probably won't say "a part of me feels this way" as often as you do now. The phrase "love yourself" will no longer mean the same thing you think it means now.

In this book, I'm going to share with you what has contributed to the creation of the fantasy of who you are. In these pages, you may read something that sparks you to come out of your sleepy trance, the nightmare of being at war with your nature, and all the misery and drama that's caused from it. You'll see how it was done to you, and how you've passed it along to others. You may feel all kinds of emotions. Some may be uncomfortable, but that is part of breaking the cycle. Breaking this cycle is the key to self-realization, and self-realization is the key to living a life that feels MUCH better.

Imagine this.

When you are born, you are clean. The core of your uniqueness, your truth, your being, is a shiny gold foundation of a house. As you become imprinted and conditioned, and are taught repression and denial of self, you begin throwing crap on top of this gorgeous foundation. You build walls from this stuff, floors, and each floor has junk piled in every corner, trash and stench everywhere.

Waking up is nothing more than removing the junk and taking out the trash. When you remove enough, the foundation is there because it's been there the whole time. You don't need to work to create it. You simply remove enough junk and there it is - YOU, in all your radiance and glory. There's a phrase I've heard often that "life is not about discovery, it's about creation." That is ONLY true when you're operating from an authentic foundation.

You can't create your life when you're pushing against yourself. You always push against yourself when you don't KNOW yourself. When you stop pushing against yourself and move into a flow, THEN you are free to create all kinds of experiences, and create them freely.

When most people start the spiritual/awakening path, what they're trying to do is to build something. But you can't build a gold castle on top of a lifetime of trash. It's like putting a rug over a pile of poo. Most spiritual teachings teach you how to spend your life spraying air freshener in the room. What I'm asking of you - if you're committed to truly waking up - is to lift the rug and clean the poo. Look at it. Deal with it. Then, you don't need to work so hard, wading through the trash and spraying air freshener for the rest of your life.

Truth and the beginner's mind

Just like in quantum physics, when you look closely enough at anything, you see that there is no substance to it. Everything that appears solid is 99.9% empty space. It is the same with the false ego. When you're not looking directly at it, all of your ideas seem solid. When you look closely, they fall apart. When your ideas of who you are have no more substance, you experience and express the truth. You let go of the illusion of substance, security, and solidness. Your truth emerges naturally and organically. You no longer put up imaginary walls and stop what is flowing, and then your nightmare is over.

11

The phrase "the truth will set you free" is exactly right. The truth is the *only* thing that sets you free. To wake up, one must let go in a way that can feel like falling into a deep abyss that, in the beginning, may mean losing everything. You may lose friends, partners, money, and status. You may lose these things because as you wake up, you may recognize that you have created everything from a completely false idea of who you are. If you're not willing to lose everything, then it is impossible to attain an experience of truth, freedom, and bliss, because you're attached to what you know and what's familiar. Your way to your bliss may be full of a temporary but painful separation from all that you think you know. You will have to have a trust and embrace a beginner's mind.

Even though all of this is temporary, as everything in life is, the desire for things to be predictable and secure is the very thing that keeps you trapped. What's on the other side of this temporary destruction is a feeling of eternal peace and flow. On the other side is true freedom, the freedom that comes from a pure expression of that which you are, a life without irrational fears, phobias, and emotional repression. Waking up is an experience of *being* that which you have been for your whole life, and feels natural and effortless.

The only way out of the nightmare is to embrace what feels, in the beginning, like an even bigger nightmare. But it's temporary, and on the other side is truth and liberation.

Why would you want anything else other than liberation? Is what you're holding onto so amazing that you would keep yourself stuck in a loop of feeling not good enough and trying to prove that you're worthy? Are you willing to see whatever needs to be seen, do what needs to be done, to live in a way that feels good? If so, then you will be liberated.

Discovery and destruction to freedom

There are two distinct elements to waking up and self-realizing. The first is discovery. You must discover who you really are, which I'll talk about more later in the book. I promise, it's not a mystical or esoteric concept, it's actually quite clear once you understand. The second is destruction. This is the falling away of the false, which I'll also go into great detail about. Discovery + destruction are the keys to living free, as an awake person expressing what's in your nature.

I'm only here to speak directly to you if you are feeling the truth in my words, to offer you a guiding hand that enables you to move through this journey with more grace, support, and insight designed to wake you up at any moment so you can live as you were meant to live.

These words are not meant to sugarcoat things in any way, because that would keep you living in your nightmare. I'm here to be as blunt as possible so you can awaken as fast as possible. Awakening is like a brush fire, destroying old foundations and spreading in a way that brings a freshness to the world, an end to insanity and a beginning to the age of thrival, prosperity, uninhibited expression, and essential evolution.

You have picked up this book because you are seeking to wake up. You are aware, on some level, that you're living in a nightmare. You have a knowing deep inside that the way your life is being lived right now is not natural. You *know* there is more. That is the voice of truth guiding you right into the deep end, asking you to trust the process. You have realized that there is no way out, only through. You've exhausted all of your air freshener, you've run out of energy, you're tired of fighting, you've burned through all of your quick fixes, and you're ready. You may be scared, but you're ready.

Are you ready? Are you willing?

A willingness and a commitment is all that's required. You will hardly find anyone awakened who wasn't 100% committed to awakening. The journey looks different for everyone, but the commitment is always there. The commitment comes from a realization that nothing else is more important than truth, because a commitment to anything other than waking up to truth means that you will remain identified with some type of not-enoughness.

Waking up dissolves not-enoughness. If you spend your life feeling as if you are not enough, all of your choices will be based on that and you will never have any lasting peace. Period.

That commitment is what creates a willingness. A willingness is a crack in a door, with a light shining through. A willingness to face your biggest fears because you are <u>done</u> being controlled by them. You are willing to let everything go, even though you have a screaming voice in your head saying "Nooooo! You don't

14

know what's out there!" You have courage. That's good, and it will serve you well. You'll need courage to put one foot in front of the other.

The good news is, with every step, you'll find your fears disintegrating one by one. The more you glimpse the truth, the less courage you'll need, because you won't feel nearly as scared as you do right now. Courage is only needed when there is fear. It is my intention that you live a life where the need for courage, as you need it today, becomes a thing of the past.

The moment of transformation - the moment it really begins for anyone - is when the known future becomes more terrifying than the unknown future. Right now, you have woken up enough to know something isn't right. You know that you're stuck in a familiar, prison-like existence. This is the first and most essential step in the awakening journey. Now you know. Now *that* you know, yes, the known future *should* be more terrifying. When you see that you're in prison, the most natural response is "Oh shit, I'm in prison!" It goes *against* your nature to be in prison. You are meant to walk free!

However, even though you may hate the prison, you know it well. Prison can be a relationship you don't like or don't want to be in anymore but you know it well, and you're afraid to be alone. Or a job that you can't stand but you need the paycheck. You know who you are in that "cell." You know where everything is. You have been taught, programmed, beaten down with other prisoners telling you to stay in prison, to fear the outdoors, to fear the sunshine, the possibilities. Ultimately, you've been told that prison - that stinking cell - is safer than the

15

unknown. You've been conditioned, over and over again, to believe that you would be better off remaining in that prison than truly living your life.

What a bunch of *horseshit* that is.

You agree, right? Good. Then let's continue.

2 Understanding Your Prison

The first step to getting free from your prison is to understand why you have created it in the first place. The prison is created through wanting to feel protected and safe, and buying into the illusion that the known, the familiar, is the way to do that.

Throughout this book I'll use the word "ego," and what I mean by ego is the *false you*. The false you is nothing more than an image that you've created in response to a belief that you are not enough or unworthy in some way. The image is constantly trying to prove itself worthy, to overcompensate for the worthiness you imagine you lack. That's it. This drives you into making choices, building relationships, and forming a sense of who you are, on top of a foundation that says you're not enough. Then you feel you need to prove yourself in some way, because you're broken or unlovable which is, of course, completely ridiculous. Let's take a closer look at how this false you that feels not-enough creates a prison for itself, and why.

First of all, the false ego wants survival. When survival becomes the objective of life, then seeking what's known and predictable is the result. This of course, is in total conflict with reality, which is that everything is constantly changing. All of life is cyclical. In nature, we have constant and regular cycles of birth and death. In our bodies we have new cells being born and others dying constantly. Everything is moving and changing all the time. Nothing else in nature fights this.

Where it all starts - death and survival

When we seek to survive, what comes with that is a fear of death. What I mean when I say "death" is "change." Every time something changes in your life, something dies and something is born.

When you emerge from the womb, the you that floats in liquid dies, and the you that breathes air is born. When you learn to walk, the you that needs to be lifted and carried dies and the you that is free to explore is born. For each new experience and growth, something needs to die. Right now, you have many ideas, beliefs, and self-concepts that *must* die for each one of these births and new experiences to take place. Your life is a cycle of birth and death, death and birth, every day. Nearly every cell in your body is in a constant state of birth and death, all the time. When you want nothing to change, you are at war with reality, and you suffer needlessly.

Let's look at it this way: In a calendar year, you see nature dying and being reborn, right? Are you terrified when a tree loses its leaves? Do you take the fallen leaves and go try to glue them back onto the tree? If you look at the tree and you try to prevent any changes, natural as they may be, then you'll spend your life trying so hard to keep the tree the same that you'll exhaust yourself. In fall, you'll be scurrying around furiously with your ladder and glue, crying for every leaf that falls, screaming that this is not the way the tree should be! It should have leaves, dammit! To allow the change to happen is much more in flow with reality.

If you saw someone gluing leaves to the trees in fall, what would you think? You would say, "that person is insane!" and you would be right. That is pure insanity. That tree is ever-changing, as are *you*. When you try to hold on to an identity that doesn't change, it's like trying to tape back on the hair that falls out of your head and the skin that sloughs off. It goes against ALL of nature.

So in one way, the ego's quest for survival results from a fear of death, or change. Another thing that happens in the quest for survival is that we unknowingly carry throughout our entire lives the same "survival needs" that we had when we were babies.

This is what can totally prevent us from having any kind of freedom.

The main survival needs of babies and small children are bonding and security (in the form of food, shelter and the like). The truth is, we don't *need* these things later in life the way we did when we were babies, literally to survive. You actually can stay alive without bonding or security.

When you're a child, you must be cared for. Humans aren't born fully developed, being able to walk and feed themselves. You are born, literally, needing someone to take care of you. You need to be safe and sheltered, you cannot do this on your own. You need to belong to some kind of grown adult to create a bond that is strong enough. If we didn't belong, most of us would have been thrown out the window by our sleep-deprived caregivers before we could walk! To care for a baby, you *must* bond with it deeply to deliver the immense amount of care that a human requires. You MUST have someone bonded with you in some way to survive.

To survive - to stay alive - is what many of us are still trying to do, without stopping to ask, "Wait - do I still have the same survival needs I did when I was a week old?" Of course you don't. You're an adult now, capable of caring for your survival needs very easily. Survival (from this basic child standpoint) should not be anyone's main objective in life. At a very early point in your life, you should have been guided into a new objective: Thriving.

But, it's impossible to guide a child to thriving when the parents know nothing about thriving themselves, because only a person who was raised to thrive - or is awakened - can do this for another person.

Shifting Focus

Because humanity has not been aware of this, we never grow out of our childish survival needs. When we're concerned with survival, we are focused on "getting" our needs met. We focus on gaining approval. Belonging to a community. Being secure and able to predict the future. We then begin, every day, to twist ourselves into some kind of pretzel: *maybe if I'm this shape I can get attention or approval and get my needs met?* We are told from society, from our parents, everyone, what it is that makes us acceptable. Instead of exploring our nature ourselves, we seek instead to adapt to surroundings, with no concern for our unique expression, no thought of thrival.

With the awareness that a focus on survival is not the main objective of life, it's important to say that survival, obviously, is important. An instinct to survive is inside of you and is operating without any need for effort on your part. You have an instinct not to walk into a situation that is threatening to your survival. When you're driving and something is coming at you, your instinct is to swerve and keep yourself out of harm's way. It's something inherent, like breathing. That's why I say you need not focus on it as the objective for your life. Life has built that into you.

The rite of passage into the shift from the survival objective (literally - to stay alive as something that is a daily concern) to the thrival objective should happen very early in life. Ideally, adults should simply observe a child's natural curiosities from the moment the child becomes mobile. Only being concerned with survival when there is real danger of the child dying. Most of the things that parents say no to is not about keeping their child alive, it's about keeping them from being hurt in any way. It's about keeping them from experiencing pain, fear, or frustration of any kind, which is a key to learning about the world, and no parent should interfere with a child getting hurt, experiencing consequences from particular actions. As long as the child's life is not in danger, a parent should not interfere.

Children are a lot more resilient than parents give them credit for, and following a child around all day saying "no!" squashes natural curiosity, learning, expression, creativity, flow, and the

21

development of individual genius and individuality. This goes against what most everyone was taught about parenting. It goes against what most of us experienced as a child. Society tells parents that are not constantly interfering that they are a bad parent. A parent who allows their child to scream in the grocery store gets put down by society. A parent who teaches their child repression and fear is celebrated. It's incredibly backwards to a natural development of a human.

The Parent Trap

Most parenting involves imposing from the beginning. Parenting should be nothing more than every day watching, observing, being curious and learning "who is this person? What are their interests? How do they work?" Then, doing their best to provide guidance and opportunities to nurture *that* person and those interests. When a parent begins imposing beliefs and perspectives of life, they teach the child, who needs them to survive, that getting their needs met depends on gaining the parents approval. This can go on for a child's entire life. From good grades and a certain type of education, to activities, to relationships, a parent says "this is what you should be." Most people literally build their entire lives on trying to gain their parent's approval, even at the ages of 60+, without even knowing it. Because of this, a person tries to convince themselves that they are "this" only to find themselves anxious, miserable, and bogged down by fear their entire lives.

In a child's most formative years, not one person got curious about THEM. Instead, they were molded like clay. Then, molded pieces of clay grow up, and do the exact same thing. They make all the choices for their children, because they've been taught that as a parent, your JOB is to make choices for your children based on what the parent thinks is best for THEM, and the cycle continues. How can we make choices for another person when we've never stopped and gotten curious about who they are?

Now, here you are, not only well past your formative years, but with having built an entire life believing that survival and approval are the most important things. That was NEVER the point of life.

Perhaps now you can see why, in most cases, a destruction of all that you have known is part of "waking up," which is way of cleaning the slate, and starting from your unique nature which was never examined when it should have been. This is all waking up is. Clearing the crap out that was never you, it was imposed upon you, by other prisoners who didn't know they were in prison. It's time to go into deep examination of your SELF. When you see the self, you wake up. That's all waking up is: The awareness of the self. Then, life takes on a new feeling and can become about what it was meant to be. Thriving in your unique way.

You'll be taking a look at some of the intricacies of the false ego and how it gets perpetuated again and again. It's my intention that by seeing this clearly, you have the capability to step out of the insane systems and structures of the world, and begin being part of the natural order of life instead of resisting it.

Through this book, I will take you on a journey. I invite you to read this slowly, absorb every word and allow it to seep into every nook and cranny. We'll look at every rotten crap brick that you've got on top of that gorgeous gold foundation. The closer you look the more it will disintegrate. We'll look at your true foundation as well, get curious about it, allow it to guide and inform you, and wake you up so you can roam free in the world.

These words are here because you have called them forth. All of these words are open to your own unique interpretation, so allow them to sink in, watch your heart open, and pay close attention to the insights, realizations, and feelings that emerge from deep inside of you.

3 The Truth About "Needs"

What if you had NO needs? Allow me to explain.

This is a simple shift in how we define what a truly actualized life is made of. I say "you have no needs" because often, when we think "I need this" it comes with a natural assumption of "I don't have this, therefore I need it."

When you spend your life thinking that you are *in need*, you live in a way that feels empty, consistently looking for that which you need. Your focus is on getting. You want to get your needs met. Or you feel that your needs are not being met. Either way, you're looking outside of yourself for another person, situation, circumstance, or object to give you something you need. If you don't feel that you're getting what you need, you focus on not having it.

Because of the way we mainly think of needs as something we don't have, and something we MUST have, this is how our false ego keeps us chasing our tails with the hope of fulfillment in the future.

The root cause of the birth of the false ego is a backwards idea I'll be sharing shortly, but the motivation for it is: survival. Of course there's nothing wrong with wanting to stay alive!

However, the false ego has a totally insane story of what it needs to survive, a fantasy that actually produces stress, disease, and conflict.

What IS the false ego?

I invite you now to suspend what you think you know about the "ego." What you've read in books, what you've learned from other teachers, and how you've come to understand what the ego is. I ask you to do this now because one of the key placeholders of the false ego is defending itself, and if you're coming into this chapter thinking that you know what it is and how it works then it will be impossible to absorb any new ideas.

The false ego keeps itself in place by feeling it knows things. A simple understanding of this is all that's required. I invite you now to repeat this simple phrase out loud, "Perhaps everything I know about this is wrong. I am open."

What I'm here to share with you is open to your interpretation, and chances are some of it will resonate and some won't. To be a responsible student you'll need to sift through the input of others to access your own truth (I will go into great detail about this later). The best way to do this is to approach every teaching with a beginner's mind, holding onto nothing you think you know. Then, go through it later, bringing in other pieces that you've learned to form your own unique perspective. I'm not asking you to take my truth as your truth. I am asking you to open up to let it in now, so you can even feel what's resonant and what's not, by letting go of needing to "defend" anything. If you catch yourself doing that, just repeat the phrase "Perhaps everything I know

26

about this is wrong. I am open" and you'll find what works for you.

Let's begin with the difference between false ego and true ego. There's a lot of talk in the world of personal development and spirituality of "get rid of your ego," and I'd like to throw a couple of ideas into that conversation for you to consider. Let's begin with a basic definition of the two:

The *false* ego is the personality that is constructed in response to a belief that one is not enough, unworthy, unlovable, not good enough, etc. It is a false image of yourself that doesn't actually exist. It's an identity that's full of overcompensation for that particular flavor of not-enoughness that you carry. The false ego is made up of beliefs, actions, thoughts, responses, reactions that are all on top of a foundation that is FALSE. Literally - not you. Not even close, in some cases.

The *true* ego is simply your actual core genius, particular traits, interests, and expression, even personality. It's who you are as an individual. It's you as the particular expression of the spirit, the source - that you emerged from.

The false ego is created in response to having everything imposed on us as children. We create a false identity that's in alignment with what our parents, families, authority figures, even those societal norms based on where we live that were not only modeled for us, but told us who we *should* be. Because of this happening day in and day out in our most formative years, we pay no attention to who we are, how could we? Instead, we are taught what we should do, how we should behave, what we

27

should value in life, what our aspirations should be, how the world is, what's possible, how we should think, look, feel, even what we should eat and drink, pretty much everything that is associated with what we call "our identity." We learned early that if we follow our own curiosities we will be rejected, shunned, and judged - because that's precisely what happened.

Children as property

Children are seen as property of their parents, and should take on the identity of the parents. We have no idea of our own inclinations and interests, instead we begin young, convincing ourselves that what's been imposed on us IS who we are. Parents teach us that to win their approval we must do what they think we should do, and if we do otherwise we will be punished. This way of relating to the world causes us to adapt a belief that molding ourselves to our surroundings is the most important thing. A child never has a chance or an invitation to do otherwise.

We decide early that to survive we *require* that adaptation. For instance, an artistic person who is born into a family that values business is told their interests are the *wrong* interests. A highly curious person who is born into a family that never questions anything tells their child to stop asking questions. Our inherent genius is never discovered or nurtured in any way.

So begins a lifetime of trying to "be something." This person ONLY knows how to *try* to be. This is why the false ego is always looking toward the future, hoping that in attaining that which you are trying to be there will be some kind of peace,

28

fulfillment, or happiness. In most personal development, spiritual teaching, or self-improvement courses, a person is not taught to discover and explore their true nature, but to attempt to change their behavior in some way so they can "be" better, more successful, or more peaceful. Instead it's just another version of these same messages we've gotten from the beginning: you need to be "this" to be liked, loved, or valued.

The measure of our worth

Because of this teaching, we get the idea that we are worth nothing, that our *only measure of worth and value is what another person places on us.* Of course the only thing that we ever get from others is what they're projecting, because only someone who sees themselves clearly can possibly see another person as they truly are.

Then, what happens is we begin to value the *image*, because we've only been taught to value the image rather than our own truth. We then hide, repress, and deny anything that doesn't match up to that image. We hide our thoughts, feelings, and curiosities from ourselves and each other. Our families taught us this because it's all they knew, and you've done it to others because it's all that you have known. This way of viewing yourself and the world is then further integrated into us through the collective - the way societies work, and what they value.

The deeper origin of the false ego is...

One of the origins of this type of imposition is rooted in religion, which is an effective way to control a society. Religion says that this lifetime is temporary and short, and the real prize or punishment comes after you die. In order to avoid an eternity of punishment and pain, we must spend this life repressing our natural desires, behaving as we've been taught to behave, and living our lives in accordance with a set of rules and beliefs that determine if we are a good person. God loves you - but ONLY if you spend your life proving your worthiness *(because you were born unworthy)*, that upon coming into the world you are a sinner and you need to spend your entire life atoning for it.

This caused a repression of emotions, sexuality, creative expression - even being unique was considered a bad thing. It was admirable to keep your head down, work hard, speak softly, and obey. Anything else would send you straight to hell. Even if you didn't grow up in a highly religious household, just know - these beliefs shaped your entire society. With this set of beliefs, how could any parent who loved their child allow their curiosity and genius to flourish? If they let their child do what was in their heart, they would go to hell, be rejected, not fit in, or be unsafe. Well-meaning parents were trying to save their children from pain, so imposing beliefs came from an idea that loving their child meant telling them exactly *how* to be a good person, *what* to value, *what* to accept, and *what* to reject.

The root cause of the creation of the false ego, is simple: *Humanity has <u>completely misunderstood</u> what God really is - and most importantly - what God is NOT.* Humanity believed that God asked, demanded even, for them to push against their own nature in order to prove their love. If the love wasn't proved to satisfaction, then God would punish you in some unimaginable way.

In short, humanity created a false ego because we believed that God *asked us to.*

In the United States, the Christian religion was part of what this country was founded upon, so this is no surprise that we've now got this way of doing things that if left unexamined, keeps perpetuating itself. Even though many parts of the country have begun to think differently about religion, we, collectively, still find ourselves raising children in the same way: Please me, or be punished for it. Parents unknowingly took this on, asking children to be more concerned with doing as they wish than by exploring their own nature.

Now you may understand how and why you were imprinted and programmed. I invite you to *let go* of being mad at your parents for it, and let it go if you are a parent. In *this* moment - YOU can begin looking in the direction that will bring you freedom and liberation. People only do what they're taught to do, and you can't beat yourself up for what you didn't know, what you didn't have access to.

In this moment, right here, right now - YOU are breaking the cycle that has kept humanity in chains for centuries. Celebrate that. Examine, gain knowledge, test that knowledge against your own experience. Awaken your curiosity. Look closer at how "things are done" and ask yourself, "Is this working? Does this make sense? Am I, and others, thriving in this system? Do I feel at peace, expressed, and whole?" If you look closely you'll see the answer is an emphatic NO. Repression and stress lead to disease, addictions, anxiety, depression, and a life lived in fear.

31

We have repression and stress because we are, in every single moment of our lives, pushing against our own nature, our own genius, our own wisdom, our own truth.

Open your eyes and get curious

If you simply open your eyes and look, you'll see. You don't have to look any further than in your own mirror. Waking up does not require magic or mysticism. You do not need anything other than a single OR collection of enough moments of clarity to snap you out of it. In my experience, there is one simple thing that leads to a true and lasting awakening: Curiosity. That thing that got squashed out of you. Being curious, asking plenty of questions, walking through the world asking, "Wait - why is that the way it is?" You begin to do this enough and every concept that you've ever taken as "truth" will fall apart. Then you can really begin to live.

I invite you now to get curious, and focus all of your attention on the point that is most critical to your awakening, evolution, and even the ability to truly enjoy your life: YOU.

4 Exploration of the True Self: Self-Realization

What is self-realization? It's often defined as living fully in one's potential. This is impossible when you don't know who you are. Over the years, I've seen a lot of spiritual teachers talk about your "true" self and being in touch with your "divinity," and that self-realization was to *realize* your divinity. Which, in a way is true. However, those words and concepts left me with more questions than answers. Now that I'm finally experiencing what self-realization actually is for me, divinity seems a LOT more accessible than they way I was holding it in my mind.

I moved to San Francisco, CA when I was 32 years old. San Francisco is the land of new-agey, hippy, free-love kind of thinking, and I had a lot of access there to many different types of spiritual teachings. A few years after being in California, I was introduced to the Law of Attraction teachings, and that led me, with my natural curiosity, to dive in head first into all things spiritual. I tried to look the part, talk the part, and meditate and do yoga like a good proper spiritual woman.

I tried SO hard to get in touch with 0my true self. I mistook my "true" self for someone who was very different from me. I thought that my own way of being was wrong. I thought that my "true self" would match up to that image of the spiritual person who was pure, sweet, nice to everyone, never got angry, thought and spoke only positive words... you get the idea.

I realized that most everything I was learning *never* brought me anywhere close to self-exploration. Instead, I was being taught that I had the power to create my life, I could have whatever I wanted as long as I focused on it hard enough. The problem was, everything I wanted (and I didn't know this at the time) was bubbling up from my false ego, and not my individual nature. Most of these teachers were selling right to my false ego, which was so busy trying to get something, anything, that led to some experience of completeness. I was trying to create from a fundamental feeling of lack.

"True self" is not an esoteric concept!

Self-exploration leads to seeing and experiencing your true self. Your "true self" is *not* an esoteric concept. As a matter of fact, the way you'll learn about "true self" here will probably be a huge relief, because it will be something that actually makes sense. Real world sense, not some airy concept.

I have been a life coach for several years. I discovered a process from years of coaching and began creating what I call a *Core Genius Map* for my clients. I had no idea when this first was created that it would be used for self-realization. I simply was creating this map to offer a way for my clients to choose a business or career that was a good fit for them. Looking even closer at what this is - I realized how this map is so much more powerful than simply choosing the right professional path, but it can illuminate a person's life path.

In all of my years of focusing on self-realization and awakening, I never truly knew what it was apart from how enlightened teachers described the experience. I can see now that in creating this map for others, it opened an awareness for me that wasn't there before, and was a key component in my own awakening. This map revealed one's true nature and inherent genius, and because of this, one could finally lean into what came naturally to them instead of pushing against it. Then, a real self-realization could happen.

People would come to me when they felt stuck in their lives, and I could see that what was causing them to be stuck was this idea of who they "should" be, period. They really didn't know who THEY were. How could they choose a path that would be fulfilling when they weren't aware of their true, inherent genius, or even their true interests? Or, if they *were* aware of some of them, but had spent a lifetime rejecting and denying what came naturally to them? I saw that most people felt stuck because they couldn't seem to get out of the patterns, ideas, and beliefs they had created as a result of striving for an image. But there was a voice inside of all of them that knew there was something more. They weren't sure what, and that's why they came to me, to find answers those questions.

Years ago, I would listen to someone tell me who they were and what they wanted, and then I would attempt to help them create it. What I found over and over was that they would have so much resistance to creating what they wanted, and it was a very frustrating experience to witness. We would then focus on "removing blocks" and other (what I now refer to as) garbage, hoping that we could fix what was in the way. Of course this hardly ever was effective long term. I didn't know why at the time, but I learned through not only watching what was happening in my own life, but asking a lot of questions and getting very curious as to what the issue really was. In reality, there are no blocks when someone truly knows, owns, and flows with their genius. All the blocks come from trying to be something or someone they're not.

Core Genius Mapping - the "me" that's been there all along

As my own journey progressed I saw how childhood imprinting and conditioning was causing a false ego to form in childhood. So, instead of asking my clients who they were and what they wanted, I began to dive deeply into their childhood imprinting. As we uncovered more and more, I not only saw who they were *trying to be* and why they were stuck, but what their nature and genius really were. Then, I was able to create that map for them, and I watched something miraculous happen. In every Core Genius Map reveal session, my clients all said the same thing: "Wow - that's always been there, all along. That's *me*." THIS is what I call SELF-Realization. Instead of some *concept* of self, you can see clearly who you are - and when you see that clearly, you can stop resisting it. This is all waking up really is - the resistance ends because you stop fighting with reality, you stop trying to create a fantasy you.

This is what should have happened to you in childhood - to have someone pay close attention to who you were. Then, as a guide for you, they could give a name to your interests, reflect back YOUR genius, and point you toward resources to help you develop, hone, and express that genius. Self-realization. Nothing magic or mystical required.

That is the way to connect with YOUR divinity, which is to explore that individual genius deeply. That is the best way to honor your creator, by being that which you were designed to be, not by squashing, resisting, and suppressing God's perfect design. Letting flow that which wants to flow. Expressing that which feels good to express.

Your divinity is located in your inherent genius.

If you want to feel God's presence, experience that which God created in its full glory. YOU. Upon full self-realization, the false ego melts away, because you see the truth: YOU are much BETTER than anything you've been *trying* to be. It's easier, much much easier to be what you are than trying to be someone else!

Whose dream is this?

When this happens, you can move into self-actualization, which is taking the "being" (realization) and moving it into the "doing" (actualization) which creates rich experiences, and those rich experiences are what life as you know it is all about. *Experiencing* that which you ARE.

An example of this is a client I worked with. In the beginning of our work together, she told me that it was part of the life she wanted to create to live alone out in the woods. She didn't know what she wanted to do exactly, but she knew this for sure. Had I

37

helped her create that life of isolation, she would have designed something that wasn't her dream at all.

What we discovered when we looked at her imprinting was that was her mother's dream. She actually was well-designed to be in the spotlight in a way, surrounded by community. As we looked at the false ego she created, she learned to fear the spotlight in any way because of a father who told her directly, and also demonstrated with his actions, that she was not to outshine him in any way. Her childhood imprinting led her to deny her own nature. As I looked deeply into who she was, and was able to give names and witness to it, she realized who she was, and shining brightly felt more natural to her. The life that she began designing then was something that felt very fulfilling, exciting, and purposeful. Had she not had a curious eye gaze on her, she may have spent her entire life pushing against herself. This is a vital step in full self-realization. You can't go with your own nature if you're unaware of it.

You will find your divinity, your genius, in those things that feel easy, those things that have been there all along. Your genius is revealed through those natural interests that you have. However, you learned a long time ago that those interests may not be the right interests, or, depending on the weight of your imprinting, you may find yourself so disconnected that you're not even aware of what your interests are.

This denial of your true nature is a simple thing to detect if you look deeply into your own life experience. When you recognize the ways you're pushing against your nature, and the more aware of this you become, the more "junk" gets cleaned off of your shiny foundation. Absorb it all and use this as a guide to explore yourself deeply. It's just as vital to your self-realization to see the lies as it is to see the truth. If you can't recognize a lie you can't recognize what is true. The false ego is a total and complete lie that doesn't exist, that never existed, is nothing more than a fantasy in your imagination. It's no different than photoshopping yourself in ridiculous ways that you can never be, and then spending your life beating yourself up and trying every day to be that image of you that's a foot taller with green skin. As hard as you try, you'll never be that. You spend your life fighting a war with a phantom.

Let's look deeply at the phantom for the purposes of recognizing it as such. When you can see it with crystal clear clarity, you'll be one step closer to dissolving the false you for good.

5 Exploration of the False Ego

Chances are you've spent the majority of your life feeling like your false ego *is* you. The false ego is, as I said before, created in response to feeling as if you are not enough. You then attempt to create an "image" which is enough - and because you are pushing against your nature, it results in the stress, anxiety, conflict, depression, and repression that have become the standard norm in most cultures. This is because the false ego, the "not enoughness," has become so normal that we've built most societies on it. Because the false ego is an illusion, and it is SO normal, on a mass level it's easy to see that we value illusion much more than truth.

The collective value of illusion over truth

For example, let's take a look at the government of any society. The sane reason for a government makes sense. Elect someone who can speak for and represent a group, someone to be the group's voice, and make sure that the concerns, requests, and collective needs are accurately communicated. Because this person is elected, it would be someone that the group trusts to speak for it when making policy decisions, as well as to communicate accurately and honestly back to the group. The government would then be a group of elected officials that are all coming to the table with the intention of finding ways of living, distributing goods and services, and the basic functioning of a society that work best for the whole. Well, that's the sane version of what a governing entity is.

Obviously this does not match up with the reality. This is a result of the collective value of illusion over truth. This is what happens: Each of us has our own phantom image of what we're trying to be. That image is a flawless, spotless human who is always a good person - a person who looks a certain way, acts a certain way, and believes a certain set of beliefs and so on.

Here is how valuing illusion shows itself in a government: A person becomes an elected official. Generally speaking (in the United States anyway) we want a man, most of the time a white man, who is clean-cut, married, has children, got good grades in school, is successful and has money, blah blah blah. Someone who looks idealistic. Then the public puts him under intense scrutiny. If that man has ever cheated in any way he is awful. If we catch him in a lie we don't trust him. We expect him to be perfect. The irony is that the impossibility of this expectation actually forces the politician to be phony, to keep secrets, and to lie or order to be this illusionary image.

I've often said that a properly elected official would be a person who, at some point, had hit a very painful rock-bottom in their lives. THEN found a way back on their feet, and now has a new self-awareness that can only come from such an experience. This person would have been to hell and back. They would have come face-to-face with the lightest and darkest sides of themselves and

41

their society. With that new awareness, a natural confidence would emerge. Then, perhaps they discovered a strong desire to give back something of value to their community. THIS is a person who can speak for all that a community is, and knows its deepest needs as well as its greatest possibilities.

Many times we elect leaders who are white and male, which only represent a small part of our society. In reality, we elect the 1%, and then turn around and are surprised that they sought out politics to gain control and power. Then we wonder why we feel that we are at war with our governments. Because we *are* in a sense. They don't represent the whole of a society, but the *image* that a society has of itself.

This is the same war we have each day with our *own* image of who we think we should be. When we have that war on a micro level, we create it on a macro level.

Under the thumb of the false ego

For instance, we celebrate and value actors, celebrities, and professional athletes to ridiculous proportions. We pay (value) some actors millions of dollars for a few months of work, and we pay (value) the people who contribute education, care, and the services that are essential to the functioning of society a wage that keeps them on or below the poverty level.

If you open your eyes, you can see what a society values - escape, illusion, and entertainment as well as image, status, and all the things that the false ego feels it needs. Interestingly enough, we hold our celebrities to the image they project. If we,

42

as the public, find them doing something that's not living up to their image, we publicly crucify them for it. It's like a celebrity who's portrayed as the "girl next door" having a drug problem or something like that. Interestingly this is the exact same thing we do to ourselves.

You try all day, every day to live up to the image that you (unconsciously) created, and then every time you do, say, or step one foot out of alignment with that image, you beat yourself up for it. You want to be good and kind, but dammit you got angry so then you say to yourself, "How could you?" You want to be a good listener but uh-oh, you talked too much! "You should be ashamed of yourself" you say in your mind. You want to be non-judgmental but you just gossiped about your friend. "You're a bad person" that voice at night is saying over and over.

This kind of thing goes on most of the day, nearly every day of a person's life. It consumes our lives and causes so much pain. Then, we try to get out of pain. We take pills, go to healers, form addictions, eat, or watch tv. Sometimes we seek out therapists to "fix" us, because clearly we're broken. We pay for programs that tell us they'll "remove our blocks" to having a life that matches our image of what life should be, and on and on.

All of this is because the false ego says you are worth nothing, *that your only value comes from that which your parents, society, even God itself place on you.* It says that you must earn love, that you have needs which others must meet, that you are fundamentally incomplete and the only salvation lies 20 feet ahead. You never actually catch it, and even if you do attain something you may find yourself feeling good for a fleeting moment, but it never lasts.

The false ego says that you are right to prefer your current known misery over the unknown future. The false ego says it may not work out, so all day long you try to do affirmations "I am successful and have everything I want!" and of course the only reason you need those affirmations is because you are scared you can't have what you want. How could things be any different when you are identifying as incomplete, needy, and/or worthless?

Life now or salvation in the future?

Often, in spiritual teachings you may hear some version of desire being the root of suffering. It's one of those things that can be very easily misunderstood, and cause someone to confuse desire with expression, creation, and evolution. I'm going to offer a translation of that statement, *"when you live your life believing that the future holds all of your salvation, you suffer."*

We, again, can trace this back to most organized religion which actually encourages repression and promises that if you do, you'll have salvation in the future. This becomes a perception of how life works. We have a desire for things like money, fame, and romance because we feel that it will make us happy. Most of the time the desire is born from present unhappiness and dissatisfaction, from not having and desperately needing. *That is the desire that causes suffering.* The desire birthed from not enoughness. The desire itself then becomes a constant reminder that we are lacking.

When you become aware of all of this, then you can consciously or unconsciously begin a quest to *eliminate* your ego, fight it, or try to integrate it. However, when you try to get rid of it, you are confirming that it's real. The false ego is nothing more than a fantasy. I've written it many times already, but it's important to keep reading it, to keep hearing it. It's not real. It's a dream. A bad dream. It's *not real.*

That's why self-realization is called "waking up." It's waking from the dream, the nightmare of a false you that is wrong, bad, and broken. You are none of that. You are a genius at being you. If you feel like something is wrong with you, it is a sure sign that you are *misidentified with a figment of your imagination.* Even if you don't know what that means yet, I invite you to consider that you, the real you, never feels broken in any way. It has no need for inferiority, insecurity, or phoniness of any kind.

Practice this:

Put your hand on your heart each time you feel that desire to fix yourself, and say, "What if this isn't real? What if there is nothing to fix? What if everything I think I know is wrong?"

These type of questions open portals in your mind, and bits of truth can begin to seep through.

When the truth comes in, the majority of fear goes away. Just consider the impact of that.

45

In the next chapter, let's look at some specific examples of genius and individuality to make this even more real for you.

6 Self-Realization is NOT One-Size-Fits-All

I absolutely adore watching talent shows. In the last few years with the televised talent shows, I watch them and often feel a swell of emotion rise in my whole body. To me, it's such an awesome way to look right into the eyes of the divine. I love seeing people with these enormous classic talents like singing or dancing, as well as some of the more obscure, not-so-obvious talents that are expressing creativity and ingenuity in a way that just blows my mind. As I watched the last episode, all I could think is: *this is humanity in all its glory.* It looked to me like everything divine that I love about humans. Each person was SO unique. To me, it's a moment of witnessing God in full expression.

God in full expression

There are those of us who don't sing well, can't draw a picture to save our lives, and I'm one of those for sure. I have some of the not-so-obvious talents, but over the years I've come to have such an exquisite reverence for them. I have no patience or raw talent to paint or sculpt. I can dance a little bit, even twerk with the best of 'em (especially after a cosmo or two) but the talent that goes into choreographing a gorgeous dance number will always elude me. As for a musical instrument, not really my forte either. I'm

47

also smart, but certainly not Einstein or Will Hunting smart. If I measured genius by IQ standards, or talent by certain artistic standards in any way, I would have said that I'm not talented and most certainly NOT a genius. Upon redefining what genius was for me however, I found that I have plenty of unique-to-Anastasia talents, genius, and creativity in every nook and cranny of my being.

One of the talents I possess is a gaze, a watchful, intense gaze of curiosity, appreciation, and awe. I have talent for reflecting back to someone in such a way that it lands and penetrates them deeply, because I can offer another attention in a way they've rarely experienced. When I take the time to learn about someone I offer them the gift of being seen in a deep and complete way. I have a gift for appreciating the beauty in someone else. When a person has their genius witnessed and revered in a deep way by another human, it can become unleashed. I am a genius at finding, recognizing, and reflecting the genius of another.

I also have a genius for taking complicated concepts and breaking them down so that people can understand them. This comes very easily to me. I have a way of grounding ideas into real world feelings and pictures. I have a genius for communication, inspiration, and bold expression.

You are witnessing me, self-realized and growing more each day. This is nothing more than the recognition of that which is me. Another person who is self-realized is someone you may find singing on a stage. Someone else who is self-realized may be designing a computer chip, cooking a beautiful meal, or playing baseball. The possibilities are infinite. An awake, self-realized person may sit quietly in the corner, or talk passionately for hours. They may stand on a stage inspiring people to rise up, or tell jokes that bring laughter to the room. You may see an awake, self-realized person acting or directing, teaching children, or living in a cave in Tibet.

THIS is what I mean by exploring your genius and your nature. Looking deeply at those things that you just do or even gravitate toward. Your genius may also be something that's ever-fluid and undefinable, perhaps it's part of your individual genius to be free, travel, and experience adventure. It could be in another's genius to grow deep roots and be closely connected in their communities, maybe even bring people together.

Awake is different for everyone

The problem with putting self-realization, enlightenment, or awakening as an image in your mind is that the image *never* matches the reality. It can be a slippery slope to read or listen to any enlightened teacher talk about enlightenment. It's difficult, if not impossible, to keep your mind open if your teacher is telling you exactly what you will want, not want, or what it looks like when a person is self-realized.

The aspect that I and other awakened teachers can agree on is that your false ego is no longer there. As far as the YOU that remains, you will be as unique as a fingerprint. You can be awake and not even be remotely "spiritual." You can be awake and do any ol' thing you want to do. Awake doesn't look like something specific. Awake is different for everyone.

There's another myth that waking up/self-realization requires some kind of mystical experience, and that if you don't see angels in your room, talk to dead people, or regularly travel to another dimension, you can't wake up. This is complete nonsense. Some people are mystics, some aren't. Often, the mystics, who have access to and are reporting on the more subtle energies of the world, can often confuse mysticism with being spiritually awake.

Waking up is the dissolving of the false ego. That may indeed happen during a somewhat magical or mystical experience. It may happen after 10 years of meditation. It may also happen in the checkout line of the grocery store. If you've never had a mystical experience, no worries, you will still wake up if your priority is truth. If you have had them, groovy, because you are here to remind the rest of us that there's more to our world than we can detect with our physical senses, and that's a part of your genius.

I knew a woman who was bursting with talent. Literally bursting with it. She had a beautiful voice, wrote songs, played instruments and loved to be on stage, and was also a brilliant actress. Early in her life, she dove into spirituality and absorbed the teachings of many different gurus. She lived in ashrams, shaved her head, and started meditating all the time. One of these gurus told her that expressing her talent made her arrogant, and the desire to be on stage only came from her ego. Those words penetrated her like a knife through the chest, and she immediately felt ashamed of what came naturally to her.

She then began focusing all of her effort on desperately hoping to wake up. She believed that upon awakening, she would be sitting still, full of bliss, expressing nothing. I remember at the time how I saw that her desire to wake up, in her mind, required that she deny her talent. She tried to hide it but I often could see the pain in her face. She tried so hard to look, sound, and behave like one of her gurus, and repressed so much that she would often have explosive and seemingly out-of-the-blue tantrums. It was easy to set her off.

Beware of false idols - or egos

For her, the quest for awakening *itself* became a false ego. She consistently pushed against her nature, trying and trying to become the woman in the image. Every now and again I would hear her sing, and in those moments it was easy to feel how high her energy and vibration were. The resonance that coursed through her veins came out and filled the room. None of her gurus encouraged her to explore and express that which came naturally to her.

Today, I invite you to take in a new meaning of what self-realization and awakening is. It's not going to look like anyone else's. You will simply cease to be at war with yourSELF. This is leaning into the *flow* of life. There is nothing more sacred than witnessing someone who loves and appreciates their qualities. We have confused humility with self-deprecation. Humility is *not* about acting small, quiet, and keeping your head down. Humility is nothing more than having a pure reverence for who you are and that which created you.

A person with humility can not only be up on stage spreading whatever their light is, but appreciate yours as well. A person who stands up in their life and says, "I've been given great genius, and I *honor* God by expressing it and being that which I am."

A rose blooms because it IS

The purpose of arrogance is to take from another, because the root of arrogance is in inferiority. It is *not* arrogant to shine. It is with *only* utter humility that one can shine the brightest and be the most expressed, for no other reason than the natural pleasure of shining. It's not about getting anything in some manipulative way. Ironically, when we shine for shining's sake, we receive in the purest way.

A rose doesn't bloom for the purpose of arrogance. A rose simply blooms because that's what it does, and the **bigger it shines, the more sunshine naturally can touch its petals.** You work in the exact same way.

7 What Self-Actualization Is, What To Do, And What Not To Do

Once you realize, then you actualize. You make choices, take actions, and cultivate your entire life experience as a natural expression of that which you are. Realization + Actualization = a fulfilling life that flows as it was meant to. Upon realization your resistance melts away because you cease the war with reality, the fantasy dissolves, and you organically move into actualization and experiencing that which you are. It's one thing to know that you have a genius for creating art. It's another thing to actually create it. In the experience of creation and expression, what's inherent in your nature is when life is truly lived.

In order to "do" you have to "be"

I'd like to share with you here a little bit about why it can be difficult to self-actualize, and a bit about my experience in moving into self-actualization. In many cases, people try to actualize something without doing any real exploration. Basically, what this means is wanting to be *doing* without the *being* to back it up. This is what a lot of personal development focuses on - altering behavior and hoping that if you can just stick with the behavior long enough that a change will happen on the inside.

Trying to alter behavior does have its merits, and it actually can be effective in helping someone change something that's not working. There are entire industries out there of people who can help you to stay accountable and make plans and agreements, all designed to help you change from the outside in. Personal training is a good example of this. You hire someone to help get you in shape and hold your hand through the process, and if you stick with it, you can certainly feel better.

It's not as simple as saying that working from the outside in isn't a good thing to do. It really depends a lot on what it is you wish to change, why you want to change it, what kind of difference you believe it will make in your life - and if it will actually work to do that.

If you're wanting to be in better shape, have more money, have a partner, be famous, start a business, whatever it is - there's nothing wrong with those things. However, when you are *trying* to actualize, which is bringing something in your dreams into reality, it's wise to take some time to question what you're seeking. Not from a judgmental place, but from a place of curiosity. Are you wanting to lose weight because you feel that you need to to be accepted and loved? Do you want more money because you feel that it will bring peace? Are you wanting to be famous to gain attention? In many cases, there's a motivation driving the desire to actualize that's rooted deep down in not-enoughness. The big disappointment is that often, once you get those things that you felt would make you happy, the feeling is short-lived.

What <u>really</u> gets in our way

There's also something interesting that happens when someone wants to create a situation or circumstance without doing any exploration into who they are. You try to create whatever it is, and then you bump up against some type of resistance, obstacle, or fear. Some people call them "blocks." At that point, instead of getting curious about who you are and diving deep into that, you may then focus all of your attention on trying to eliminate what you feel is in your way.

It looks like self-sabotage, but in reality you're never *really* self-sabotaging and you have no blocks. That's never the point of what you're trying to do when you stop yourself. It's easy to understand why it seems like you're self-sabotaging, and the intention to go and remove a block, change your mindset, or eliminate resistance comes from a good place.

However, now all of the attention goes to what you feel is wrong. The exploration itself is tainted with the intention to do away with something. I've seen people spend a lot of time, energy, and money on this step. There are many programs, coaches, books and teachings that are targeted to helping you push through your fear or obstacles. At first you may even feel empowered. But this is exhausting, and at some point you get tired, hungry, sad or angry, your guard comes down, your willpower runs out, and you feel like you're stuck back at square one, wondering why creating what you want feels so hard to do. This is what happens when we try to design a life for ourselves that's not based on knowing who we really are.

There is nothing to fix

There's a belief that every "new level" or, to be more accurate, every *change* in your life is going to be met with some type of inner or outer resistance, and you'll need to overcome that resistance (which will be painful) and that's it and you should never expect anything else. No wonder it feels hard to grow or change in any way. I can speak from authentic experience that this is not, in any way, one of life's inevitabilities.

One of the few traditional spiritual teachings that I have actually experienced is "what you focus on expands." However, I have a bit of a different perspective of this than what is commonly taught. When you focus on obstacles, it's not that they literally grow, it's that the act of focusing on something means that you are *identifying it as real.* You fail to see the illusory nature of the "obstacle" because you declare with every moment that you are going to give your attention to it, that it is real, and it is in fact in your way, and in order to move forward you *must* work to remove it. If you don't remove it, you will remain stuck and be forever unfulfilled. You give all of your power to the obstacle, which is a figment of your imagination. This is why it doesn't work. Again, you are at war with *reality.*

Here's an awakening opportunity for you, right here and now. Look at your reality. Is this working? Is focusing on your obstacles getting any lasting result? Maybe at one point it did. But then you came upon another obstacle and another one.

From this moment forward, put no more attention on removing blocks, obstacles, or resistance for the purposes of making your life work. I know it may seem scary, you may wonder what will happen if you stop focusing on the problem, when everything inside of you says that your only chance at salvation IS to focus on the problem, otherwise you won't solve it. This is the moment where you can look at the REALITY vs. the illusion.

My question to you is: *if focusing on the problem really worked, wouldn't it have worked?* You don't need to take my word for it; instead, simply use these words to point you to something that's painfully obvious once you have the courage to look right at it.

Pushing against your nature

Most chronic painful situations in life, whether it be physical pain, poor health, struggles with money, relationship issues - all of it - if you look closely enough at them you'll find that in some way you are pushing against your nature. The *only* real way to deal with a challenge in any intelligent way? Turn a curious eye on learning who you are and how you work so you can see what's really going on. Stop trying to fix "what's wrong." There is nothing wrong with you.

One more time: if you want to actualize, express, and experience who you are, you *must* be aware of it. If you are running into perceived obstacles, that's why. There's more to discover about yourself. Loads more. The time to invest in self-realization will be the most wisely spent time in your life. I see so many people who believe that they don't have the time to do any self-discovery, they need to get everything in place before they invest energy in that.

Without knowing it, we collectively view getting curious about the self as some kind of luxury, something that can wait until we make enough money, get the kids out of the house, find an extra 5 hours per week in the schedule, get the grass cut, the bills paid, the laundry done and lose 10 pounds.

Awakening moment: do you see now, in this moment, how insane that is?

People can lose thousands of dollars and years of their life trying to become the person they think they *should* be. If they spent a small percentage of that time on discovering their true nature, then it would save them gobs of time, energy, and money and put them on purpose a lot faster, with an undercurrent of peace inside. Self-realization is NOT a luxury. If you are tired of life feeling so damn hard, then your focus on revealing that which you are is a *wise* focus. Then, you can truly actualize.

Since I can only speak from my experience, I'll share a bit about how I experienced actualization. The moment my false self was gone, the resistance was gone. Another strange feeling was that I didn't "need" to do anything. The "shoulds" were gone. I no longer needed any of those things I thought I needed. For a few days, I didn't really do much of anything. It was lovely to sit and feel the sensations of calm. I no longer was filled with anxiety. I no longer needed to "be someone," I needed no validation from anyone, and I didn't care about being noticed or seen. I didn't call my friends and tell them this happened, and since that's all I ever talked about for years, I found it to be funny that I didn't care to announce it or talk about it right away.

But then, in a moment without thinking or planning in any way, I began to write this book. I was flooded with ideas for my business and the way I really wanted to work with people. I didn't go sit on a park bench for 2 years, I only sat on my ass for a few days. Then I *wanted* to move, not because I should, but because it just happened. Each day I felt it more. The more I wrote the more I knew what to write, and it unfolded naturally. Motivation wasn't an issue.

For the first time I was experiencing expressing for expression's sake and creating for creation's sake. I was doing simply what came natural to me, I was *actualizing* those things that had been there all along. The lie my false self told me was that without her, I wouldn't motivate. I would be a loser. The truth is she was killing my *real* motivation, because I was only motivating from not-enoughness. I was free to choose. I felt a freedom to just go live in a van down by the river, or be an international speaker, or go work at a coffee shop. All of those options became ok, and only in that moment could I notice what was naturally arising in me, now that it had nothing keeping it shoved down in any way.

I moved naturally into actualizing without having to force myself or "stay on track" or be disciplined or any of that. Because I no longer needed any of it and wasn't attached to being defined by success or status, I was able to create something that was simply a natural and organic expression of me. I have no resistance to the flow of life because I am not defined by something outside of me. This is my experience of what self-actualization is like. It's only here on the other side that I can really see that there were _never_ any obstacles and that my false self was nothing but a fantasy.

Moving into true abundance

To put your focus on the truth is wise. It is true that if you seek you will find. There also will come a day where the seeking will end and the expression of life, uninhibited in any way, will begin. You move from destruction to expression, and you begin to experience something amazing. You move into the experience of true abundance.

Abundance is misunderstood to mean "a lot of," and in reality abundance is something much bigger. When you begin expressing your genius from a self-realized place, and you're expressing for expression's sake, you become open to receive more than you can imagine. You don't need to "try" to receive, it's a natural flow that happens without any effort on your part. When you realize that you have all that you need, you simply recognize that the problem was never that you can't receive, but your false ego kept you from feeling it. The false ego is rooted in lacking, so as long as you're identified with your false ego, your "not-enoughness," lacking will be your experience.

Abundance is a force that is there, all the time. It's an endless supply of energy, resources, information, opportunities, nourishment, and love. When the illusion that you're not enough dissolves, a new kind of evolution begins. You simply recognize that you ARE in the flow of something incredibly abundant. As a result your genius starts developing, changing, growing, and sharpening. The more it grows, the more your expressions evolve, and it continues a cycle of growth and evolution, ever-changing and ever-flowing. You begin to experience what life really is, effortlessly. Your energy becomes powerful and vibrant, you begin to have access to more wisdom, resources, and awareness.

Actualization is a connection with the flow of abundance, which is an experience of giving from overflow, because you are no longer feeling that you lack...anything.

From this point forward in the book, I'll dive into more specifics and intricacies of the components of self-realization and awakening. I cannot know all of your journey or what your exact path will look and feel like, because you are a unique person. I can however, invite you to explore your truth deeply, shift a perspective or two, and have a few ahas that can lead you to discover something of value.

I am one simple, but essential, stepping stone in your journey. You wouldn't be reading this if there wasn't something important here for you.

It's a vital thing to mention here and now: you must run this through your own experience. Never ignore your own experience. That this truly is the only thing that matters. Feel free to lean into what resonates and pay no mind to the rest. You will gain something or open up in whatever way you're ready to at this time. Trust the process and notice what insights, inspiration, and ideas occur to you.

8 The Power of Radical Honesty

Now we're going to deep-dive into some real aspects of waking up, and to be radically honest with you, pretty much all of these are uncomfortable. There's no way to avoid looking at that which you've hidden from your consciousness, because to do that keeps you stuck in the loop of illusion. Take a breath, and one by one I invite you to explore these different topics and notice the experiences that come with them. Your path of waking up will be yours, for sure. Remember what I said earlier about willingness? If you're willing to do this exploration, you will find your truth, revealed to you along the way.

It's appropriate here to tell you a bit about what I was like before awakening, especially a few years back. I felt so broken, unlovable, not good enough, and I had this idea that I was unwelcome on the planet. It was from there that I created my false ego, and it affected every moment of every day.

Because I felt so awful deep down, I began to find interesting ways to overcompensate. This was all unconscious at the time - I had no idea I was overcompensating, I just thought it was who I was. For instance, I was extremely arrogant and I always felt inferior or superior to another person. Because one of my core genius elements is communication, when that genius was rooted in inferiority, I could be very manipulative or harsh. I was a master at laying guilt on people. I pushed away everyone because I was so afraid that they would see how broken I was (or thought I was, anyway.) Even when I seemed happy, there was anxiety looming underneath like a boulder I was tethered to. I struggled with depression, loneliness, and suicidal thoughts. I actually attempted suicide in my 20's, twice. Needless to say, I had a lot of miserable days. Most people had no idea how much I was suffering, because I did my best to hide it from everyone. I was deeply ashamed of it.

In 2014 I had what I now call the awakening *before* the awakening. This was a life-shifting realization in which I could finally see not only how "asleep" I was, but that my life would be much easier if I stopped pushing against myself. I didn't know who I was yet, but I knew that what I was trying to be definitely wasn't it.

This is the point at which I was introduced to that liberating force called "radical honesty." It wasn't about telling my friend that, yes, she did indeed look fat in those jeans. It was about looking inward, deeply inward, at all the ways I was lying to myself, and also the ways that I hurt others as a result of it. This was not fun, not even a little bit. But, it was hands-down the most liberating, freeing experience of my life.

Radical honesty, for me, was like eating crow every single day. If you don't know what eating crow is, it's defined as: *Humiliation by admitting having been proven wrong after taking a strong position. Crow is presumably foul-tasting in the same way that being proven wrong might be emotionally hard to swallow.* I was dining on a steady diet of crow for a very long time.

The most painful part of radical honesty was the initial sting of shame, anger, or sadness that came with everything I owned up to myself or said out loud to another. To realize that I manipulated another human being for purposes of getting something I felt I needed, to realize that I belittled someone for the purposes of lifting myself up, to realize that I was insanely jealous of someone and secretly wished for them to fail, that I preached one thing and practiced another, all of the lies I told, oh the list goes on and on. I could fill a book with just that.

I could understand why people *didn't* want to wake up. This is the part of waking up where you are looking at all of that stuff you built on top of a belief that you are unworthy in some way, which makes us all do some horrible things to each other and to ourselves. I don't know many people that can bear to see this. We all want to feel like we are noble, and it's others who are awful. We are good and others are bad. We are the ones who give, give, give and it's others who take.

Trust the process - take it in steps

This kind of honesty, for me anyway, came in steps. All at once may have been too shocking to my system. I learned at some point to trust the process, and to not push too hard. I would own what I could and what I was aware of at the time. The more I did it the more I was aware of, and in the final weeks before my awakening I was able to access some very deep stuff, but by then

I had an association between radical honesty and liberation that had built up through time.

Also, the more I did it, the more I realized the sting of guilt, shame, or embarrassment was temporary. It was only there for a short time and not only did it not kill me, I built up a bit of a tolerance to it. What used to bring piles of shame now only brought a spoonful, so I could go into deeper places and slowly cleanse out more and more. It was never fun, and I never enjoyed it. But I *did* enjoy the effects, the relief I felt to just be aware of it, the little transformations that happened as a result, and the freedom that I noticed.

I was chipping away at my false ego little by little, looking so intently at it that it began to lose its grip on me. My ego told me I would die if I saw this, said that, and let go in any way. Through experience, I learned that it wasn't true. I recognized the voice that kept me in prison, and how it kept me there. I didn't die. I actually felt better. Over and over. Lo and behold, the truth was indeed the opposite of the lie! It took courage because I was afraid, terrified to see these things in myself. But I had reached the point of being so miserable I saw no other alternative.

Your journey will look and feel different from mine. I chipped away at my false ego brick by brick. One *big* part of my false ego was anchored in needing to being right about everything all the time - a way of overcompensating for feeling small, stupid, and not enough. Because of how my particular ego was showing up, eating crow was one important part of my awakening journey. For someone else, it could be boldly stating what they believe, and that may be the path that opens them up to their truth. For others, it could simply be feeling and acknowledging their feelings.

But you see, practicing radical honesty will be part of your awakening in one way, shape, or form. *You cannot wake up if you refuse to let go of your image.* I could describe radical honesty as the <u>mortal enemy</u> of the false ego. You cannot keep up your image if you're beginning to get honest with yourself and others, and look at that which you are afraid to see.

This is the way to experience ultimate and total vulnerability, and what it feels like to be open in a way that you've been not only wanting to be, but protecting yourself from your whole life. To walk through the world from an open place is, in reality, not scary at all.

It's much more scary to relate to the world as a dangerous place from which you must protect yourself, and that's the one aspect of the ego's rationalization for maintaining its image.

The reality of life is that it is indeed much more frightening to *fear* the truth than to face it. The sting of radical honesty is very temporary. The fear of it keeps you trapped in a false-image prison your whole life (remember that stenchy can full of trash hiding the gold?).

The only thing you ever really have to lose is that prison. There's a whole world outside for you to play in, and it's waaaaaaay more fun than that damn cell. It's liberation. You can breathe, move, dance, create, love, and so much more.

Radical Honesty in action

In conversation and relationship, radical honesty could look like taking responsibility for yourself in a way that is, indeed, radical. It's looking at another person and saying things like, I hurt you, I used you, or I gossiped about you because I feel small or wanted attention. In other conversations radical honesty may look like revealing things like, I am struggling with money, I am unhappy in my marriage, I resent my children.

Even admitting those things to *yourself* is challenging, but to reveal them to another is another extra crispy layer of challenging, because in those moments you let someone see behind the image, behind the perfect life it looks like you lead on Facebook, and open yourself up to judgment, criticism, or rejection.

Radical honesty for you may mean expressing anger when you're angry, sadness when you're sad, or anything in-between - even when your false ego shouts: "No! Don't let them see! You'll die if they see! You'll die if you're rejected! You'll lose everything!"

For now, the awareness and the value you put on the power of radical honesty will guide you. You'll be presented with plenty of opportunities (especially now after reading this!), and this moment is one of them.

I invite you to spend some time contemplating this for yourself before you move on to the next chapter. You can begin any way you like; you can journal, talk to someone, or simply think about it. *What are you hiding that you're currently aware of, and why are you hiding it?* That's a question that will get you started and will open you to seeing things more clearly.

Often when realizations come up, there's a feeling along with it. Sometimes it's shame. Sometimes it's anger. Sometimes it's sadness. This is very important to allow these feelings to be there, since they are in reality, because there's so much that's been repressed for so long, and this is part of a cleansing process.

Remember, emotional repression is the biggest and most destructive form of stress that exists in our world today. Life always has temporary stressors which happen to all of us. Your body is built to handle those well by supplying bursts of adrenaline, raising your heart rate and signaling your body to be on high alert. Nature designed you with the resources to deal with stress. This way you can keep yourself safe and deal with problems that *require* a certain amount of stress to supply you with the fuel you need at that time. It's part of that inherent instinct for survival, and is there without you needing to be aware of it.

Emotional repression creates long-term, consistent stress. If you take a piece of wood, and put even a low level of stress on it for long enough it will break. In a society full of false identities, nearly every single person, including you, suffers from some type of emotional repression. Collectively, this has become a normal way of life, to be "stressed out" nearly all the time. There have been all kinds of things that have popped up over the years to help us cope with stress, become more mindful, and relieve the tension. Most of these things just provide a temporary effect, if at all. So you can imagine the destructive effect on your body over time, the near-breaking level that the high-alert adrenaline supply is causing.

It's not only our childhood imprinting, but there's also collective imprinting that can affect us on a larger scale. For example, and from a general perspective, *(and this is truly general, there are many more nuances than I could possibly list)* many women are raised to be quiet, look pretty, smile, and focus on being attractive. This could cause women to repress any power, anger and tension to uphold the image of what she considers attractive and acceptable. Many men are taught to be strong, stoic, practical, and not show emotions like sadness or fear. They then repress anything that they feel makes them look weak, undesirable, or undependable. These kinds of collective images start as children - "Boys don't cry!" and "Good girls aren't bossy!" - and seep their way into the identities we create, and the reason we unconsciously choose to repress.

Repression is nothing more than a side effect of a false image of yourself, and collective imprinting is just what happens on a larger scale. However, it's important to look at this very closely because emotional expression and cleansing are a HUGE part of waking up, and this focus is another great way to start practicing radical honesty, right here, right now.

Detoxing Your Feelings

As you honor those feelings they will dissipate on their own, and I strongly encourage you not to "try" to get to the liberation part.

That must happen on its own. Imagine the discomfort you feel as nothing more than a much, much needed detox, letting out some of what's been suppressed little by little. Just like a detox, you can't hurry it up, you just let it happen. You also can't decide when you're detoxed fully and when to feel energetic - that just happens as well. You'll feel it.

Tune deeply into the truth inside of you and it will always remind you to trust the process. Then, when you begin experiencing some much needed relief (like after a good cry), you'll know there's nothing to be afraid of.

9 There's Gold In Them There Triggers...

Stepping deeper into the pool of radical honesty, you'll find lots of triggers, which are absolute *gold* in the waking up process. I know, it's not exactly fun to look at this stuff. But you know what IS fun? Expressing yourself and living your life authentically without some not-enoughness stuff holding you back. When you run from triggers, you're missing out on a direct path to waking up a *whole* lot faster, because of what they reveal. Some of these things that piss you off are pointing you directly to the subconscious beliefs and perceptions that once revealed, can be questioned - which is how you free yourself.

What is a trigger - and where is the gold?

A trigger is something that gets you *really* worked up and often comes as an uncontrollable knee-jerk reaction. Triggers can reveal what your particular false ego is trying to be or trying not to be, based on what it believes, which can lead to unconsciously projecting onto others. Triggers can also reveal what you're suppressing, and if you look closely - triggers can ALSO reveal some of your core genius. Pretty much ANYTHING that a trigger reveals is something absolutely amazingly valuable to your self-realization.

Triggers are nothing to be ashamed of, run from, or avoid in any way. Imagine that what triggers you in some way is nothing more than a messenger, an angel messenger, here to show you exactly what is keeping you from liberation. This angel messenger knows how to get you out of prison! Triggers are awakening gold, rich treasures that, unfortunately, most people won't look at.

There really is beauty in all of the things that get you worked up, pissed off, or sad. Looking into them is a way of seeing so deeply within yourself that you can see through the lies, and right into the heart of the divine inside you. Let's approach triggers as our friends who want nothing more than for us to see who we really are, so we can live as we are meant to, and find out where they lead.

When you look at something "out there" that causes a knee-jerk reaction, it takes courage to look at the source of the trigger as you (more accurately, the false you and the perceptions that it has). This is hard only because turning the focus back on yourself is one of the most threatening things you can do to your self-image. It's also the MOST liberating and will wake you up *because* it's so threatening to your self-image. This is truly where the rubber hits the road in the awakening process. It's truly a balance between discovering who you are - and dissolving of what you aren't. As you start to observe this, you'll see a lot more about how triggers show up and what you can really learn from them.

The most courageous thing any person can do is to reflect on this, so remember what a badass you are for even being willing to contemplate what I'm sharing with you now. I know how challenging it is to see this stuff, but it's so *incredibly* worth it, I promise you that.

Projection - a big source of triggers

Let's begin by looking at what projection is, which is a huge source of triggers. Projection is a defense mechanism, and happens when you project your beliefs, repressed thoughts, or feeling onto others. When you begin to witness yourself projecting, in those moments, you ARE waking up.

Think of projection literally as a movie screen in front of you. Imagine now that there's a movie that's coming out of you and being projected onto the screen. You can see what's on the screen clearly. However, what happens to most people is that they're unaware that this is coming from them. They see it on the screen and believe they are witnessing something outside of themselves. They believe it's something that they're looking at and taking in, instead of projecting outward.

Now, here's the really nutso thing that we humans do. So we're projecting our own stuff on a screen (or a person, situation, or circumstance in front of us) and then, we react - even get thrown into an anger or rage about what we see. In some cases people spend their whole lives in this loop: project outward, get triggered by what they see, and try to change or throw rocks at what's on the screen. It's similar to looking in the mirror while wearing a yellow sweater and getting triggered that the reflection is wearing a yellow sweater! Then, begin screaming at the reflection that if it was a *good person* it would be wearing a *red* sweater.

As more frustration builds, that the image in the mirror just won't change, then either one of two things happens. Either you start throwing rocks at the image, trying desperately to destroy it, or you feel a sense of hopelessness or depression, utterly defeated that despite all of your best efforts that damn image isn't wearing a red sweater. This is why when you open your eyes and see clearly, "OMG! That's a reflection of me!" in that moment, you are focusing on the source of the projection and not the screen. That's the only way out of the cycle.

Projection is a way of "defending ourselves" from thoughts or feelings we can't see, don't want to admit to, or repress. We just put them on something or someone else instead. You've probably witnessed yourself projecting at some point in your life. You may also know how it feels to be projected upon. Have you ever been accused of something that was clearly the projection of another, and not true at all? Chances are, if you've been in relationship with other humans in your life, you've been projected upon.

Since your projections - and how you perceive on your screen the projections of others - started in childhood and have been accumulating over your life so far, then how do you know they're just projections coming from you and not reality? How do you know you have a real, honest core value or simply a false ego belief that's not true for you?

Well, you'll know because a real core value <u>doesn't cause a trigger</u>. It's simply you being you. Only something that's *not* you is going to cause a trigger. Again, this is why looking into the face of a trigger is so powerful. Because you're seeing up close the scaffolding that's holding up your false ego, and that is what's keeping you from not only truly knowing who you are, but experiencing it.

A trigger happens when you have a belief (or beliefs) that is causing you to repress emotions, suppress personal power, deny your natural gifts, abilities, or genius, or express yourself. When you "project," you look at this person or event doing something that you've told yourself is bad or wrong, and it triggers you - throwing you into that knee-jerk anger, rage, fear, or even sadness. That's why triggers are so valuable, because they're pointing you toward the beliefs that are holding you back from your natural expression *the most.* Projection triggers reveal some big, big stuff that's keeping you stuck in the prison of your false ego.

Let's start with some common examples of how the false ego creates projections, which cause triggers.

The People Pleaser

If part of your (false) identity is that of a "people pleaser" something that gets repressed is self-centeredness. The repression of self-centeredness happens because you're told (or you decided at a young age) in some way, shape, or form, that if you focus on yourself you're not lovable or valuable. So a people pleaser is then constructed in response to that.

The people pleaser maintains its image by believing that you're always giving to others in a totally selflessness way. Because you repress self-centeredness, when you see it in others, it can make you very angry.

This causes thoughts like this, which is the trigger caused by the projection:

Geez, my husband is SO selfish! What a jerk! How dare he be this way!

I'm always helping out Sally, and where is she when I need something? She's SO self-centered!

I am always there for everyone, and no one even asks about me. I give and give and give. Everyone is so wrapped up in themselves, people shouldn't be that way!

You project onto someone else what kinds of beliefs were part of your identity's construction. Beliefs like "being selfish/self-centered is bad."

Here's some gold in that trigger: The truth about people pleasers is that they give because they feel it's what they *should* do. It's not really coming from a place of what they actually *want* to do, which is where the resentment comes in. The trigger is evidence of that. So what could you discover or dissolve by realizing this?

You may discover that you have based your entire sense of worth on what others think about you. You may discover that you have been so focused outward that you don't know who you are. Then, you are empowered to question this belief: Is it actually true that you have no inherent value? That your worth is based on how much you sacrifice? Where did that belief even come from?

As you begin to ask questions, chances are the belief won't be able to hold water anymore - because the closer you look you see that it's ridiculous that you have no inherent worth! Then, you may make a decision to get to know yourself. To find out who you are underneath the people pleasing, and put some time and attention on you. You may see, more and more every day, that the more you discover, the more you know yourself, and you know what's important to you, you feel better. You find yourself able to set healthy boundaries, say no when you mean no and yes when you mean yes. You feel more relaxed. You watch all the guilt start to melt away.

Then another magical thing happens. That friend who's "self-centered" doesn't trigger you anymore. In fact, you may even have moments where you admire this in her. When she cancels plans because she feels tired, for instance, you may say, "Good for you for taking care of yourself!" This is what happens when you allow the trigger to guide you. When you can mine the gold that the trigger (angel messenger) led you to, you no longer require the trigger. You've found the gold.

The Finger Pointer

Another example of a projection that triggers, is a man or woman who stands up and speaks out passionately about how

77

homosexuality is an abomination, should be "cured," or at the very least, not accepted. The repression happens because, he or she could possibly be gay (or at least curious, which most people are) and he was imprinted with the belief that "gay is bad." What's then repressed now becomes projected outward, and anytime he or she sees someone gay is angered, probably because of the shame that they feel. They desperately want all things "gay" to disappear.

Imagine the intense imprinting he experienced as a child? How many times he must have been told something awful about gay people? Perhaps it was beat in him or her that being gay would send you to hell (or some such nonsense) and believed it? Obviously, this trigger is pointing to something that, if owned, the trigger would soon be diminished.

So, whatever we consider "bad" that we feel like we have on some level and hate in ourselves, ends up as a projection that triggers. When you look at it instead of running away from it, that trigger points you directly to all the ways you are trying to twist yourself into a pretzel in order to be loved and fit in with the world around you. If you don't see this, you will remain "twisted up" so to speak.

I've seen a lot of teachings claim that everyone is choosing their life and all of their circumstances. This is ridiculous when you simply look at how imprinting and conditioning work. If you are unaware that you're doing something, you have no power to do anything about it. With each little aha that comes with recognizing that which you were previously unconscious of, you take one step toward total and complete liberation. These triggers reveal so much of what you've built your false identity on, and when you see them, you can begin to see what is NOT true. As you begin to see clearly what is not true, then and ONLY then can you possibly see what IS true.

The Jealous One

There's also the trigger that can reveal your unowned genius. In some cases, this shows up as jealousy. Everyone experiences jealousy, yet very few come out and can admit it to others, or themselves. Just like with all triggers, jealousy can be revealing something you want to do, but don't feel like you can, or don't feel that it's possible.

For example, let's say that you feel jealous of a friend's success. You want to be happy for them, but the green is in your eyes. Instead of pushing it down, look at it. What are you witnessing? What's bringing on the jealous feelings? Is your friend doing something that you dream about, but you don't feel will work? Sometimes, it's that you may even "think" you want it, but it's something else entirely. Asking some deeper questions about what's going on can bring some HUGE insights that will point you right to what's standing in your way.

Start with you

I invite you now to think of some things that really trigger you and why. What are you ranting about either to yourself or out loud? What really gets you upset? It's very helpful to write these things down so you can deal with them with more awareness.

As you see what's written down, now ask yourself questions like:

- What is this revealing about me?

- What can I own right now?

- In what ways do I think, believe, or act the same way? What am I hiding, and how is this helping me to see it?

This is your opportunity to free yourself, and to take full responsibility. Blame no one else for your reactions or responses. Nothing that you see outside of you is responsible for your trigger. I know it's hard to believe, but it's true - there's not one other human on this planet that has enough power to "make you" feel anything.

What you see out there is happening out there. How it goes through your particular lens of interpretation is what's making you feel how you feel. This is about focusing more on what's shining through the lens instead of what you're seeing on the screen. This is an opportunity to open your eyes and see the truth about what's *actually* making you angry.

One of the best ways to offer some insight into triggers and projection is looking at some common ones and some probable causes for triggers. As we go through this, perhaps you may have an aha or two. Of course there are thousands, and each person has theirs. These are just a few examples, so you can see the trigger and what it may be revealing. This is a great tool for doing some of your own examination.

Common projection / trigger: women who dress or act provocatively

Some common causes for this projection trigger are:

You have a belief about how women *should* look, act, or dress, and chances are you were heavily imprinted or conditioned to think that way. You may have even heard some strong opinions about women who flaunt sexuality, and in turn you may be repressing yours. So when you see someone looking or acting in a certain way, you get angry because it points you straight to what you're hiding or suppressing in yourself. So you *project* that belief onto this woman you don't know (as if she should abide by it.)

What were you told as a child about women? By society? By other authority figures?

Another possibility is that this is bringing up something about being invisible or unwanted, for two reasons: one that you're watching her *gain attention* that you yourself don't feel that you can have and that you want…

or you're watching her *overcompensate* for feeling invisible or unwanted, and that could be triggering you as well.

Look closely at the rant that's going on in your mind. What are you assuming about her? What, specifically, is bothering you about her? You may find your answers as you take a closer look at your own self-talk around this.

When you reveal what the belief is, as you question it you may find that there's a wild sexy woman in you waiting to come out! Or maybe something that has nothing to do with sexuality, but with visibility or attention.

This projection / trigger may reveal something you're repressing, and/or point you directly to a core belief that your false ego is operating from, which is usually something in the family of not enough, unlovable, unworthy, or invisible. When you start to see those things, then you can begin to question the validity of those beliefs, which begins the process of dissolving them for good.

Common projection / trigger: bullies and bullying

First of all, what are you witnessing? When someone is bullying another person, you are seeing someone who feels as if they have absolutely zero power. They feel small, insecure, or maybe even stupid, strange or awkward. They overcompensate for this by attempting to take power or dignity from another person in order to lift themselves up. Most of the time a bully learns this from being bullied themselves. In nearly all cases, the worse the bully, the more they themselves were bullied.

If bullies really trigger you, you may feel you have no power, because that's *what* they trigger in you.

If you felt a genuine power inside, either bullies wouldn't go anywhere near you, you would just walk away from them, or set a healthy boundary.

When you witness a bully you may feel irritated for sure (it is irritating to watch), but you could approach the situation with compassion which would help if you're wanting to be effective in doing something about it. More importantly, this is your opportunity to look deeply into that place inside that feels powerless, and notice what kind of choices you've made as a result. What kind of messages you got as a child.

This can be a tricky projection trigger because I find that often, when people are super duper triggered by bullies, they themselves may also be bullying. Some ways this can happen:

You may be a happiness bully. When someone is feeling sad do you try to push sunshine and cheer on them?

There's also the guilt bully. I find that couples that include a bully that is more violent or emotionally abusive is a good match with a guilt bully. One says, *"You suck!"* and the other says, *"I feel like I suck, have no self-esteem, and can't make my life work because of YOU!"*

Have you tried to make anyone feel guilty lately? Have you manipulated someone into doing something for you because you were afraid to ask? For example, *"Remember that birthday party I organized for you? That was so fun. I sure wish someone would do that for me."* The point is you're still trying to take power or dignity from someone, it just doesn't look as obvious.

If you have done it to others, have compassion for yourself. This is pointing you toward the gold, and can reveal where you may feel you have no power. When you do this, the trigger, as you experience it now, will lessen tremendously.

Depending on the situation, it's very important to say here that having compassion for a bully does *not* mean putting up with shit. You can have compassion inside of you which will give you more peace, and enable you to handle the situation much more effectively.

But it's *never* healthy to allow a bully to push you around. If the bully is abusive, it's even more important to have compassion from afar, and keep yourself focused on you. That's the only way out of the bullied/bullying cycle.

Bottom line here: the bully and the person being bullied both feel powerless. The trigger most likely is revealing that belief that you are powerless, which of course, you're not. Look deeper into the powerless feeling or belief so you can see clearly what's not true - and then what is true will have space to emerge.

Common projection / trigger: Irresponsibility, flakiness, being late, or undependable.

This can reveal that you may have a belief that being responsible and dependable to others is what deems worthiness or value in a person, or something of that nature.

When you feel like being dependable is what makes you valuable, it can cause you to put an immense amount of pressure on yourself to always be someone that can be counted on by others. This may mean that you have made choices in your life that are what you consider to be best for others, but maybe, on some level, not what you really wanted.

Because of this, perhaps you've made sacrifices that you consider to be noble, putting your own dreams or desires aside, and doing your best to show up. This can create enormous expectations on yourself, as well as others. It's very easy to project the belief behind all of this: it's bad to be flaky, self-centered, or irresponsible.

When you hold this belief, anyone doing anything that resembles flaky or irresponsible, like not planning correctly and making everyone late, is going to hit you deep in your gut everytime it happens.

Where else does this show up? What burdens have you put on yourself as a result? How much stress has been caused by those self-imposed burdens?

This can also create control issues, which are usually coming from a place of wanting to feel safe. This is the place to look closely and ask yourself to get real about what you're afraid of. What if you let go of the wheel? Will anyone else grab it or will you drive off the cliff into oblivion? Will you ever be supported, or is it always going to be up to you to make sure everything runs smoothly? If you don't make sure it runs smoothly, does that mean that you're a failure?

Of course none of that is true. Being dependable, flaky, or anything of the like does not determine our inherent worthiness. This is not only a good opportunity to use this trigger to go deeper into these questions and learn about yourself and what beliefs you have that are not only creating your identity, but also what is causing you a lot of stress.

If that belief is causing you stress, it is in *some way* pushing against your nature. I wonder if there's a desire in there to have more freedom and less responsibility? I wonder what would happen if you explored it?

Common projection / trigger: politics

Drama can totally trigger feelings of powerlessness, just like with bullies.

Huge political triggers can bring up a lot of fear of having things taken away or imposed on you that you have no control over. You may see certain politicians as well as others who agree with them as controlling or oppressing you.

Another cause of this type of trigger goes back to childhood and the way you were parented. Did you have a parent who you felt was oppressive or controlling? If you have, this can form a belief that you have no power and that it's up to someone else or something else to decide your life for you.

A feeling of powerlessness over time turns into deep resentment and then eventually into rage, if it's not dealt with or acknowledged. One thing that can happen especially when you have a parent that is oppressive is that you begin displacing your rage on others, because that parent has beat it into you, so to speak, not to challenge them in any way. You not only build up anger, but learn that you cannot express it, so it's got to come out somewhere. Politics is a safe space (in a way) to allow rage to be expressed because you don't have to go up against your parent.

Now may be the time to go back to the source of this idea that someone else has a lot of power over you. Who was that person, or persons? What did they teach you about yourself? About how to relate to them? What did you learn about life, and what's possible? What choices have you made as a result of that imprinting and conditioning? Look there and you'll find the trigger.

Like with bullies, I'm not promising that when you heal that trigger you won't take some issue or another with politics. But, there's a *difference* between feeling irritated by what you're seeing and completely thrown into a rage by it. In this case, feeling irritated (in my opinion) *can* be a very awake response to watching the bickering and corruption in politics. Again, it may not make anyone happy to look at it. However, when you're not triggered you find that you have a clearer head which can give you much more productive ideas. If you're not feeling powerless in relationship to politics, there's much more you can do, if you choose to, and you'll be much more *effective* at it.

The beauty of exploring the gold

If you want to experience who you really are,   focus inward instead of outward. Looking inward when you experience the trigger is the only way to truly resolve it. *You can't eliminate the trigger from outside of you.* Even if you are able to tell someone who's triggering you to stop doing whatever is bothering you, it's only a matter of time before it just pops up somewhere else, and you've missed a huge opportunity. Focus outside of you only to gain some clues on *where to look* inside. Triggers are great guides for exploration. The outside world is pointing you right to the most rich and juicy places to examine inside.

The closer you look the more the lie begins to dissolve. Lies don't hold up under investigation. Detectives know that the way to solve a case, aka get to the truth of what happened, is to look for things like track record, consistency, demeanor in the suspects. The most successful detectives are the ones who are very aware that they can't get too attached to anything, and they need to remain objective. In a good investigation, too much of an emotional opinion can cloud the truth because it's impossible to see things objectively and be willing to be very wrong and throw out months of work if necessary. This is why attachment to a self-image can cloud the truth so much. If you're ONLY looking for evidence to match what you believe is true, even if you have no evidence other than what you were told, then you continue believing a lie.

This the key reason to question everything - especially what you were conditioned to believe. Conditioning and imprints can be passed from generation to generation without anyone stopping to ask if they're true, and why they're true.

The story of the Christmas Ham

This is articulated well in the story of the Christmas ham. The new bride is making her first big Christmas dinner and tries her hand at her mother's ham recipe, cutting off both ends the way her mother always did. Everyone thinks the meat is delicious, but says, "Why do you cut off the ends — that's the best part!" She answers, "That's the way my mother always made it."

The next month, they go to their grandmother's house, and she prepares the famous ham recipe, again cutting off the ends. The young bride is sure she must be missing some vital information, so she asks her grandma why she cut off the ends. Grandma says, "Well, that's the only way it will fit in this pan."

How easy it is to accept something as truth that may not have any basis in real truth - there's no evidence that the ham tastes better with the ends cut off! But when no one questioned those beliefs it was easy to adapt them and build entire lives around them. When the "right way" or the "wrong way" to be, do, act gets internalized, that is one root of a projection trigger.

Whatever you see that goes against those beliefs will give you a strong emotional reaction. That is a sign that can point you to what the belief IS, and then finally, an opportunity to ask if it's true, and examine it. When you do enough of this examination, this causes your false ego to begin to dissolve.

Looking at projection and triggers is just one way to find out what scaffolding is holding up this idea of who you are. Be a detective, and put everything you've been told up for questioning, and remember, under questioning, the truth always comes out. Go deep into the core of what's keeping you from self-realization and freedom. Just be gentle with yourself and go one step at a time. You can make giant leaps with just a little awareness.

10 Redefining Love

In terms of self-realization and what it truly is, it's oh-so-important to address the subject of love. So often, when a person self-realizes, their ideas of love dramatically shift because they're no longer operating from "I'm not enough" anymore. There are a lot of misunderstandings about what love is, what it is to love, and what it is to be loved. We confuse love for all kinds of things: lust, attraction, attachment, codependency, expectations, impositions, obedience, attention and most of all: approval.

Love is literally none of those things. What love is in reality, not in fantasy, needs a lot of clarification because the very nature of it is so radical to what you may believe it is. The more you understand the reality of love the more awake you become, and the more awake you become the more you can truly experience what love actually is.

Love is a force of witnessing and reflecting essence. To be loved is to be witnessed for who you truly are. To love is an experience of witnessing essence. Love is a liberating, binding, and nourishing force. If you were to describe what God is, you could use the same definition, and this is why it's been said that God is Love. However, since historically we've mistaken God to be a judgmental ruler who asks everyone to spend their whole lives proving their worthiness, because they have no inherent value other than what God places on them through their obedience, it's understandable that we mistakenly think that love is almost exactly the same.

The truth of God and Love are the same: Full freedom is granted, you are loved and fully witnessed by God, and your life is to do with what you will. You are fully supported in whatever you choose to do and express. There is no judgment or punishment placed on you from outside of yourself.

The only consequences are the ones that naturally occur through your expression, and are there not to punish or reward you, but simply because that's how nature works. When consequences happen that *feel* good or bad, you have the option to learn from them so that you can be equipped to make new choices and see things in a new way - or not - if that's what you wish.

Self-realization and love

This is why self-realization is *critical* to the full experience of love. When you have a false ego that is rooted in "I'm not good enough" or "I'm unworthy," then that very idea is not only internalized but projected outward. You hide so much from yourself and others that you cannot allow anyone to witness your essence, because you think your essence is lacking in that which makes you acceptable or worthy. In many cases you can become completely disconnected from it, or push down anything that doesn't fit what you think your image is. There is nowhere this can show up more than in your relationships.

What most people consider to be love is actually control, attachment, and fear. When people get into relationships, in the beginning the focus is on being accepted by the other. This is when a lot of things get hidden, pretty much anything that you believe may get you rejected. As the relationship goes on, some of that guard comes down and then it switches from wanting to gain approval to deciding whether to give it - but only if certain requirements are met. Both parties seek to have the other meet their needs, fulfill their desires, even validate their very existence. Of course because you have two people that both feel lacking and trying to "get" from the other, this is where the disappointments and arguments set in. Then one of three things happens.

Either the couple splits up, someone becomes dependent and slowly but surely loses who they are, or both parties become dependent on each other and lose who they are. This is NOT what love is.

Love...with conditions

To say that you love another but ask them to be home at a certain time every night, never look at, sleep with, or develop feelings for another person, to behave in a certain way, to not behave in a certain way, to make particular choices, to sacrifice themselves and what they want in any way, to limit or have no real freedom, to be obligated to you, to be responsible for making you feel wanted, to meet your needs, to believe certain things - the list can go on and on - this is NOT love. This is not a relationship that is based on love at all. This is a relationship based on fear.

So does this mean that all romantic relationships are based in fear? No. Relationships certainly can be based on love. If they were based on love, real love, however - the institution of marriage as it stands *today* would probably dissolve. In a true love situation, you would never promise another that you would feel exactly as you feel today and want exactly what you want today because you know that you cannot honestly promise such a thing. You would also *never* ask this of another person.

A real love relationship would be a coming together for the purposes of freedom and witnessing essence, and reflecting that essence to each other. A real love relationship would always ask the other to follow their truth, even if that meant needing to explore a relationship with someone else, leave town, change their beliefs or perceptions, or end the partnership. Real love would never ask another to suppress or deny themselves of their truth. Real love liberates, awakens, and celebrates life itself and the ever-changing nature of it.

It's very possible that a real love relationship could last a lifetime, but that would never be the *goal* of it. Imagine the intimacy that's available in a relationship that gives freedom and witnesses and reflects each other's essence? Most of the reason relationships end is because of the pain that's caused through the current fear-based nature of them. In a real love, the relationship would only end if it made sense to end it, because the truth of one or both parties *requires* that the relationship end or evolve into something else. The irony of this is that the more freedom relationships bring, the more likely they are to last. The very thing people do to make lasting relationships - demand promises, guarantees, and impose obligations - is the very thing that makes them miserable or ends them altogether.

This is what evolution and self-realization, truly look like. All that's required to evolve is to wake up and examine the reality for what it really is. That's why it's called "waking up." This idea of relationships doesn't require that you believe me, I simply ask that you examine this for yourself.

In a world that is in tune with reality, in which true love could be experienced, relationships as we know them would dramatically change. All relationships: parent-child, partners and lovers, family, friendships - all of them. This type of evolution begins with one person at a time. It begins with you, and your willingness not only to evolve your own perceptions of love and relationships, but your perceptions of life itself.

You can begin now by taking the focus off relationships with others and what they're doing for you or not doing for you, and putting it solely on yourself. In the continuing exploration in redefining love, I have another radical idea to share: In order to love another, one must become 100% *self*-centered. Yes, you read that right. Most of us are beat through and through with the idea that self-centeredness is bad, and that selflessness is good, and self-sacrifice is even better.

Self-centeredness - your greatest gift

I hear a common objection to this: "What about my kids? My responsibilites? How do I put the focus on myself when that's the last thing I have time to focus on? Won't I be neglecting my children or letting everyone down?" First of all, I'm not here to convince you of anything. If you are telling yourself that focusing on yourself is something you don't have time for, then so be it. This is your life to lead and you can focus on what you want to. I'm simply telling you the truth, which is if you want to truly love and experience all that love is, the only way to do that is to focus on yourself for the purpose of self-realization, which is the path to experiencing love as it really is.

Upon self-realization, the false "I'm not enough" ego dissolves, and when you are aware that you *are* complete, then you are able to love fully, to witness and also be witnessed. If you are self-realized then you can see your children as they are and guide them toward their own truth and expression, which is to love them in the purest way. Waking up begins with a willingness.

You can't possibly see all the steps, however, you *can* begin to recognize that focusing on yourself for the purposes of self-realization would, hands down, be the greatest gift for your children. You could realize now that sacrifice teaches sacrifice, and sacrifice leads to misery. All that's required is a shift in perception, and then life will guide you in the best way. If you even *consider* that your children could benefit more from your self-realization than from your sacrifice, then your path will unfold in a way that is perfect for you.

Love and self-love

In the exploration of love, I'd also like to offer some insight on the idea of loving yourself, which is also a different thing than most people realize. I hear this often, and a few years ago I said it myself, some version of, "I just need to love myself. Right now I don't." Let's do a deep dive and pick this phrase apart a bit. First of all, who is the "I" and who is the "self" that you want to love? And what does the loving entail exactly?

What comes up a lot when we think of "self-love" is self-care and nurturing. It may be an act of self-care to take a hot bath, take a day off, exercise or eat something healthy. It may mean to look in the mirror and say something nice to the reflection. It may be to do something that brings you a positive feeling. These things all feel good to do, and it's nice to treat yourself well. But the effects always wear off eventually and you return to whatever your default state is. If you need to remember to treat yourself nicely, then what happens in those moments where you are caught up with life? Chances are if you're needing to remember to make time for self-care, your default setting is set on self-sacrifice in some way.

In looking at the definition of love, which is freedom, witnessing and reflecting essence. When you focus this on yourself, you are led into a wonderful world of exploring that which you are. The more you see, the more you get to know the truth of yourself, the more integrated you become. You see, when you are going through life unconscious of your genius and your unique nature, you feel divided into "parts."

You feel fragmented because, in a way, you are fragmented. You're not, in reality, but what I mean is that there's a true you and a false you which we've talked about at length. When you begin an exploration of the self, the beginning of that focus is when you realize that you're identifying with something false.

You're awake enough to know that you're living a lie - which is HUGE.

This is usually when you go out looking for help seeing yourself clearly. This is what teachers, coaches, and guides can offer support with, in some cases. I say "in some cases" because actually a small percentage are awake enough themselves to reflect truth back to you. In some cases you can have a guide project onto you and guide you based on what they believe is right or wrong, which of course can lead to even more confusion.

But that's not always a bad thing. Even if you're going out and getting crappy guidance, sometimes that crappy guidance can point you toward a truth. Remember, always run everything through your experience. Ask yourself how you feel about what you're being exposed to. Even confusing teachings can spark something, you may find yourself saying, "Wow - that doesn't resonate at all! But wait, why is that? What does that reveal about me? What does resonate?"

With this kind of reflection you will always gain something valuable in every experience. Other humans can be great catalyzers for revealing your truth. The bottom line is that loving yourself is an act of deep self-awareness and exploration - and yes, other people can be helpful (if not vital!) in leading you through an inquiry and holding a space for you to fully realize what comes out of that inquiry.

Space and silence

Many teachers have said that space and silence are necessary for awakening. I agree with this wholeheartedly. You must have some space to reflect and observe. This is why experiencing love and being centered on yourself are one in the same. When one builds a life on self-sacrifice, it's easy to imagine that your schedule may become very busy in a way that accurately reflects that self-sacrifice is a good way to be. What bubbles up are a lot of feelings of guilt, resentment, anger, or exhaustion. Perhaps now you can see how much more you could not only give *love*, but experience love and all the beauty life has to offer by shifting your focus to self.

I told a client of mine once, "You can't wait for things in life to line up. You must decide what is so, what is important to you, and what is non-negotiable, and then watch - you *will* figure out a way. The path is ONLY revealed after the decision is made. You can't see it before you decide. Decide, then notice what happens." This can happen now, even if you don't know where you'll find the space. Upon an internal shift of your priorities, you'll find new insights, opportunities, and awareness that will guide you.

Love, freedom, and expression are some of the most delicious things in life. Life is not meant to be a struggle. Life is not meant to be hard. Life only feels hard to live when you're pushing against your own nature. Love is not meant to be a struggle. Love is not about control or obedience. Love is not about being who someone wants you to be, or giving your power away to another person.

Love liberates. Liberation feels like a deep breath. At first it feels like a deep sigh of relief, followed by an expansion that feels like an explosion of joy. There's a deep undercurrent of peace that accompanies you through all of life's experiences and cycles of nature, cycles of birth and death, and cycles of energy. That peace is the grand space holder that allows you to be at your highest high and your lowest low with no resistance of any kind. Life is meant to be lived in love. That's who you are. You are pure love.

11 The Little Big Things

There are a lot of ideas, even myths and legends, about what it is to be awakened, and the *right way* to awaken. There's debate among the awakened people on this. Some say that spontaneous awakening is the way to go! Others say gradual awakening is the way to go!

There is no way that's going to work for everyone, that's what I say. However, there is one big truth here - spontaneous awakening is not something you really have any control over at all. Anyone who has been through it will tell you that. You can't say, "on Saturday I will have a spontaneous awakening!" The very nature of it is that it comes, well, spontaneously.

Gradual awakening is what most people do, waking up little by little instead of all at once. I found that the more I paid attention to the each step, the more I appreciated that this was a gradual process for me. I had time to adjust to each new awareness. Spontaneous awakening, the experience in which your false ego dissolves instantly, can be blissful for sure, but also very jarring to your life. Since most, if not all, of our choices are based on the false ego's motivation of trying to be good enough, spontaneous awakening can be disorienting, and you may need a long time before re-orienting in the world.

This is why a popular awakened teacher was homeless for a couple of years shortly after his awakening. The minute he woke up all that he was doing in his life lost the meaning it had before, and he just cared less and less until he let everything go, and went through a re-orientation period that lasted a while.

There are some souls for whom spontaneous awakening works, and for others, it doesn't. In my gradual awakening process, one of the transitions I made was from being very driven and ambitious, to finding my motivation slowly but surely circling the drain until there was nothing ego-based left.

Right before my false ego dissolved, I went through a few weeks of deep depression as I had witnessed the last of the external motivation dissipate. I literally found no reason to get out of bed or do anything. It was a very hopeless feeling. Had I not been through so many steps before, I may have been more frightened or even suicidal.

Because mine was a gradual process, I knew deep down what was going on. I knew that I couldn't control it or push it in any way. I had learned through experience to trust the process.

I didn't talk to anyone much, but I did have a conversation with my mom who was worried about me, and told her that I knew that this needed to happen. I knew my final egoic motivation was drying up, and I also knew that the truth would emerge if I didn't fight it or resist it in any way.

The voice of truth

This voice of truth was a faint whisper, but that same voice had carried me through the whole awakening journey. I learned early on to respect each step and never attempt to rush anything, because I would only ever receive what I could handle. The deeper I went through my illusions the deeper I was able to go, and each stage prepared me for the next. In fact, the more I paid attention, the more I had an awe and reverence for the perfection of the process. I knew this was my unique journey and perfectly designed to show me exactly what I needed to see every step of the way.

The irony in waking up is that you can see clearly that you have always been everything that you were seeking. And then - yes, you do feel much better! That not-enoughness is no longer there. You are still there, you still have your particular qualities and what I call "true personality," you still have bills to pay and practical matters to take care of. All of that remains.

The motivation - the *why* behind your life - that's what changes. After my awakening I still sat there for a few days, but this time I was enjoying that I had no *need to do* anything. I had nothing to prove. I needed no external validation or approval from anyone. I loved sitting in this space, it was a totally new feeling. On the outside it may have looked similar to being depressed, but inside it was a mix of huge relief and a total state of peace. Because of who I am, my motivation returned, I had lots more of it, and it felt pure. It was simply me being me. I felt no more desire to run from practical matters either, in fact those were taken care of with a lot more ease. Life is now an experience of having no self-imposed obstacles in the way and feeling things just flow.

The big little things

Now let's take a look at one of the elements of the awakening journey which I call: the little big things. This is about noticing the shifts, the nuances, the transformations that are happening along the way. Some of them are so subtle it's easy to miss them. Noticing them is not only the way to wake up a bit faster, but to enjoy the journey a *whole* lot more.

This really began for me a couple of years before my awakening. I had hit a place in my journey where I knew I had gone as far as I could on my own. I had hit a wall with what I was able to recognize, and I found myself on my knees in deep surrender. I opened up to receive help from others, and some big transformations in my awareness happened as a result. I hired a therapist who did some EMDR with me, and I opened up to a lot of new awareness of some old childhood trauma I was carrying around. I also met a man named David who did some work with me around my imprinting and attachments. This is when I became familiar with the idea of "the little big things."

I was like most people when it comes to asking for help from someone. Inside there is this hopeful, eager little voice that says, "Can you fix me? Please?" I would have some amazing session, have some whopper ahas, and then I would go back into my life only to be disappointed that the same issue was still there. When I started to look closer, though, I saw something amazing. I noticed that there *was* a shift, and even though it felt small it was evidence that something fundamental had changed.

Let's say there is a situation or a person that just triggers you. Whenever you come into contact with it, it's like a knee-jerk thing that brings up the same agitating feelings in you. Traffic is a good example: You sit in traffic every day, and you always feel anxiety about it. Perhaps it's higher on certain days, but you always feel *some* anxiety. Now, imagine that you do a session with someone or have a breakthrough about the reason you always feel anxiety in traffic. It's that slap your head kind of breakthrough, and you can never unsee it again. In that moment it's hard to imagine ever having anxiety again. And for a few days you do feel better. But then, there it is again, just when you think you've conquered it - that damn anxiety is back.

Imagine that for the next few weeks, you still have that same reaction 9 times out of 10. But that 10% is now feeling *no anxiety at all*. You just sit in the traffic, maybe you don't love it, but you're not feeling that pit in your stomach. Maybe it's so subtle that you don't even notice.

But one day you do notice. You have a moment where you observe yourself and say, "OK, wow! On Tuesday I didn't feel anxious at all!" Maybe you did every other day, but that day you didn't. You didn't even have to think about it. You didn't *try* to feel calm, you just *did* feel calm. Now that you noticed, you notice more, and you watch that number go up to 30%. Within 6 months, you barely feel any anxiety at all except for rare occasions, and now this thing that caused you pain for years has turned into a calm experience.

Notice, notice, notice

This is how most transformation works. Often we have some kind of breakthrough and we imagine that 24 hours later we will never have the same thought, trigger, pain, etc., that we've had for years. Now, in some cases that absolutely happens. It's a lot more common, however, for things to change naturally over a period of time. In the scheme of things, a few months is incredibly fast for any measurable transformation to happen.

What I ask my clients to do early on is to notice, notice, notice. I tell them not to expect that it's all going to be different, but to notice the little bit that just changed organically. It's a lot like chronic pain. Something hurts for years, and then one day it doesn't hurt as bad, and at first you may not even notice because the pain is no longer demanding your attention, so you just focus on something else. Then you realize, "Wait - I'm feeling better!"

That's always a fun moment. It can feel like a crack of sunshine in a dark basement, just when you've lost your hope, there it is: evidence that *something* is working. What you focus on expands because, well - you're focused on it! It's not magic, it's reality (which is pretty magical!). When you see something you see it, and when you see it you can see it more and more, clearer and clearer.

That's why I call them "the little BIG things." They are HUGE, those little 10% shifts in thought, feeling, or behavior that required ZERO effort on your part. On the awakening journey, these are very motivating, and the evidence feels good. It reminds you that you're on the right track and what you're doing is working. It feels like a getting a gold star reward, and these moments are wonderful to notice and celebrate.

This is why taking some space to reflect is not only essential for awakening, but essential to witnessing the journey itself - all the ups and downs, highs and lows along the way. Each one of those moments reveals something about you. A genius, a talent, an interest, or even what's NOT an interest, a genius, or a talent, but what you've been *trying* to be (you know, that false ego popping up). It feels SO good to finally realize you'll never be what you're *trying to be*. You can only be what you <u>are</u>. Imagine the biggest exhale you've ever let go, the deepest sigh of relief, and the release of years of tension. It's almost orgasmic! There are a lot of these moments, and paying attention helps you to notice and appreciate them with everything you are.

Waking up also feels good!

There's a lot in the waking up journey that feels good. Even in the midst of some things falling apart, there are these wonderful moments when the rising of the truth and the effortlessness of it begin to build that link, little by little, between waking up and liberation. In those moments you'll find yourself feeling more aware, more peaceful, and more able to give and receive love. You don't have to wait until you're completely awake to have all the fun!

When I start working with clients and we begin to look at some of their imprinting and release attachments to old identities - even before we get to the Core Genius Map - they watch themselves shifting. I hear a lot of things like, "I wasn't afraid to say what I felt to my husband," or, "I said 'no' without feeling guilty," or, "I felt calmer and more focused at work." Many things shift. In many cases, ideas and inspiration start flowing, they seem to care less about what others think, and they notice themselves becoming more patient. Their communication with people in their lives deepens. They feel less insecure and afraid.

This is one of the best things about working with a coach, and I say this from the point of view of the coach and the client: being supported in reflecting on what's changing. As their trusted guide, I love piecing together what they're telling me so they can see it even more clearly. A client can talk about all of these little things, and then I'll come back with an enormous reflection for them that often sparks an "oh wow, yes, that IS big!" kind of moment. It's powerful for me to see and for them to be witnessed so accurately and completely. A lovely experience for both of us.

So, "the little things:" Knowing that all along your journey, transformation and awakening *can and is* happening, right now. All the seemingly minor ahas, new awareness, and little moments of clarity are spreading underneath the surface, through your consciousness and growing. When you notice, notice, notice, you find evidence of this and can feel good about your journey, knowing that everything is not necessarily going to change overnight. In fact, remember that what you focus on expands, so your shifts will begin to grow exponentially as you notice, celebrate, and enjoy them.

It's not about practicing patience - patience means you're waiting or tolerating the present moment feeling like the future holds your salvation in some way. This is about understanding how transformation *actually* works. Once you accept this as reality, then you can be in a space of celebrating and acknowledging the step you're on and the realization you're currently having. Then, you can really enjoy the journey and the unfolding a whole lot more! It's really quite glorious when you notice it.

12 Busting Through The Comfort Zone (Myth)

There's this idea that growth is - and even *should be* uncomfortable, and it's true and not true at the same time. I know it's confusing, but in this chapter we're going to put this phrase under the microscope a bit, because it can create a lot of misinterpretations that aren't always helpful to self-realization.

The phrase "everything you want is outside of your comfort zone" spreads an idea that being comfortable means that you are not expanding and evolving, every time you reach for something in life or do something new you'll be scared, and you need a lot of courage to succeed in any way. I'd like to shed a new light on this because there's a reason that you're scared, and it doesn't necessarily mean that fear is about simply trying new things.

Growth doesn't have to be terrifying

The truth is that evolving/expanding isn't actually scary, it's the most natural instinct that you have - and it doesn't look the same for everyone. There is no "right way." You can be quite comfortable and completely content with your life and not only still grow and learn, but do that with *zero* fear.

This is an important concept to understand, because here is what often happens: People get so used to the idea that we must be uncomfortable, or in some cases, downright *terrified,* to make any changes in our life that it's easy for us to confuse personal evolution with pushing against what's in our nature. Until you're aware of who you really are, you may not even know the difference. It's my intention with presenting this subject to you that you can start to notice the different sensations that happen when you're awakening and when you're simply going against the current of your natural and inherent genius. They are very different experiences, and it's wise to know the difference so you can step into a life that flows, feels good, and is ultimately rich and fulfilling.

Let's put each experience under the microscope a bit and take a closer look.

First, let's examine what is commonly thought of as "comfortable." In reality, comfort is awesome. The actual definition of comfort is: *a state of physical ease and freedom from pain or constraint; things that contribute to physical ease and well-being; prosperity and the pleasant lifestyle secured by it.* What's not to like about that? It's fabulous to feel a sense of comfort and ease, have a nice bed, a full belly, and a body that feels alive and vibrant. In that sense, the comfort zone is something you may feel in the sanctuary of home, where your needs are met and you feel good. Being uncomfortable in that sense may be being in physical pain, hunger, too hot or too cold, and unnourished by your environment.

It's a strange thing that in some cultures or teachings, that your ability to be uncomfortable and tolerate pain is almost revered and considered to be an achievement. Those tv shows about people who willingly put themselves in situations where they're thirsty or starving, extremely cold or hot, exhausted, and miserable have always seemed a bit strange to me! Or things like walking on hot coals, sitting in a sweat lodge, or jumping in ice water for the purposes of transformation also send a strange message. Of course, these experiences can be exhilarating and exciting, and there's certainly nothing wrong with them if that's what you're into!

There's a big difference, however, between doing those things because it's what you enjoy doing, and doing those things to prove something. Or, even worse, because a teacher or guru told you that if you *don't* do it, that means you are weak, can't succeed in life, aren't "serious" about your transformation, or some other such nonsense. There are plenty of awakened people who never went naked in the woods for a month or participated in a fire walk. These things can be interesting and fun for some, but certainly do not *guarantee* success or enlightenment in any way, shape, or form. You can be surrounded by lovely comforts and still awaken, for sure.

Suffering doesn't earn worthiness

In a way, it goes back to the idea that you must *suffer to gain worthiness*, and the more you suffer and sacrifice, the more you deny yourself, the more a reward is waiting - sometime in the future. This is not reality, this is an enduring belief system that is about fear and control. Suffering and martyrdom have long

111

carried an air of nobility. Poverty and chastity are seen as a high value of the truly spiritual and kind-hearted. It suggests that if you are surrounded by comforts you cannot access a higher realm of consciousness and connection with the divine. Can you awaken and still sleep in a comfy bed and have air conditioning? Of course!

Other than creature comforts, let's take a look at some other meanings of comfort and the comfort zone. Usually the comfort zone, according to the world of personal growth, refers to the familiar. Even moreso, what's really being implied is that you're stuck in a world of familiar stress, fear, even misery, you're afraid of change, and scared to leave your current situation which is *in reality* highly uncomfortable, to move into a life that will feel much better. This is really the experience of prison I dove into in the first couple of chapters. The "comfort" zone should really be called *prison* zone, because that's precisely what it is. There's nothing comfortable about it, and it has nothing to do with what TRUE comfort is.

This is the big problem with calling it *the comfort zone*. The phrase is confusing and is flat out NOT true at all. In fact, the reality is that your true comfort zone is being totally <u>free</u> of the prison-like existence that so many human beings find themselves in today. Inside this zone is where expansion, flow, and personal evolution can absolutely thrive!

In a lot of personal development circles, because you're so encouraged to get out of your comfort zone and get used to being *un*comfortable, you may not even realize that you're simply pushing against your nature. You may be misguided to associate fear or resistance with growth. Sometimes, resistance is there to let you know that you are, indeed, going against natural flow. If you see resistance as always something you need to push through, then it's impossible to get curious about resistance to see what is actually behind it. In reality what you're doing is resisting the resistance by *always* seeing it as an obstacle, or even demonizing it, instead of seeing it as a messenger that is offering you an opportunity to get curious about the situation. Pain, fear, and resistance can be messengers as valuable as joy and ecstasy. They may not be as fun to examine, but they can be rich sources of awareness, and awareness is the very thing that ultimately leads to a pure feeling of joy.

Outside the prison zone

Now that we're working with terms which describe the experience, then, yes, everything you want is indeed *outside* what we'll call "the prison zone." When you're not only sitting in prison but attached to staying there, you are going to be scared to death of *true* comfort, which may range from doing and expressing that which comes naturally to you, to living in prosperity, visibility, or freedom - and everything in-between.

Very few people will ever say, "I prefer prison." Most people go through their lives saying they want freedom, happiness, and fulfillment. Of course you do! This is *you living in your most natural expression*. Prison walls are built on top of a belief that you are not good enough, and that the purpose of your life is to try to somehow, and through *lots* of effort, become valuable by someone else's standards. In the prison zone, your main concern is to gain approval. This creates a life in which you are totally defined by other people, and yes, that is prison.

Coming out of the prison zone is uncomfortable for sure. It's only uncomfortable because you are questioning everything you've ever believed about yourself and the world around you. You face things you've hidden and shoved down deep inside. You may have to lose things. All of this is only painful to the false ego, which *prefers* prison. When the ego is what you identify with, then yes, each step of letting go has painful quality to it.

Coming out of prison vs. pushing against your nature

Here's how to tell the difference between coming out of prison and pushing against your nature. When you're going through the discomfort of self-realization, there are a two things you can notice that accompany the experience. First, there is a knowing somewhere deep inside that is guiding you, an underlying peace (even if it's deep down!). It may be soft and quiet, but it's there, and it has a consoling "keep going, you'll be OK" kind of quality to it. There's a sense of surrender, a feeling of letting go, of giving up the resistance.

Second, the discomfort of seeing or feeling what you've been afraid to deal with, is usually followed by a sense of clarity. This can bring a feeling of relief, joy, or bliss. For example, you discover a projection trigger and you have that initial sting of shame or sadness. Then you begin to have a realization, and you experience an elated feeling or even a deep exhale. As a result - you see things differently. You notice that your relationship with

114

the world and/or yourself is slightly or even dramatically changed. The effect lasts.

When you're pushing against your nature, the discomfort has a different quality to it. There's a sense of wanting to prove something to yourself or another. There's an underlying anxiety and often an attachment to an accomplishment and what the accomplishment will mean. Whatever you're doing can bring a feeling of happiness - but only if a particular outcome is reached. There's a sense of pushing and fighting for something. The joy of that feeling, if you reach it, is extremely short. It's an experience of, "Wow, I did it!" followed by, "Uh-oh, what will happen tomorrow?" or the like. You may not have any significant shifts in how you see yourself or the world, and the effects don't tend to last.

I've had the latter experience in what I call "seminar high." I go to a seminar, and there are all these things that I do - break an arrow with my neck, bend steel, stand up and say what I'm going to do or be after the seminar, yell affirmations, cry about the ways I've failed in life, do a trust fall, or face a terrifying situation. I feel transformed - for about a week or two. But I find myself right back to square one, or that's what it feels like. What was missing was an explorative quality to the experience, instead, it was *designed* to "push." I believe the intention is to show people that they're capable of more than they thought, which can be good for sure. But, does it create lasting awakenings, flow, and unique self realizations? Not in *most* cases, but some.

The important thing to remember here is to notice your experience. If a trust fall or fire walk helps you to suddenly trust the flow of life, take a bold action and feel peace that lasts, then that's awesome! It's certainly worth a try and can even be a fabulous feeling. It depends a lot on your expectations, who you are, and what your particular journey entails - and it's important to try things that you're drawn to and see what you notice.

Bottom line: You *can* be physically comfortable and still wake up. When you do self-realize, you also can grow and evolve without all the fear and resistance that you experience now. In fact, when you know who you really are, you'll finally see the truth - that growth and evolution are in flow with your nature. There's no need to push. Expansion is natural in the universe. There is a constant expansion that happens effortlessly because that is the reality of life.

13 The Power of Compassion

Compassion is a vital companion on the self-realization awakening journey. Compassion turned inward can be experienced as objective curiosity, deep insights, and a welcome space for you to experience an array of emotions. I'd like to share with you how I define and experience compassion, because there are many different associations with this word.

Looking for the cause behind the effect

The way I experience compassion is simply looking underneath the surface and seeing the cause behind the effect. For example, you may find yourself judging someone else's behavior as bad or wrong in some way. Then, you may learn a little bit more about them and their background, and you find that you can feel a genuine connection and empathy, even if you don't agree with the behavior.

Imagine that you find out someone has been stealing from others. It's easy to say "That's wrong! They're a thief!" Then, you find out that they were abused, kicked out of their home, and were destitute. They were stealing out of desperation because they were cold and starving. In that instance we can see that it's not as simple as judging that they did something bad, and therefore they *are* bad. Yes, they did something that may have been harmful to someone else, but we can feel a sense of empathy and understanding that they were in a situation in which they felt they had no other choice, and under different circumstances they would not have committed the crime.

To experience compassion for another is an act of love, because you are witnessing essence. Essence: the inherent nature of a person that is *not* the behavior. Let's get real here - who hasn't done something they wish they hadn't? We've all done things that we're ashamed of. We've all done things we wish we could take back, but we can't. We've all had moments where we're in a fragile state, feeling angry, exhausted, overly stressed, or traumatized. In those moments we are capable of doing things that we would never do in a state of wellness. And we hope that someone will see who we are underneath the bad thing. We all crave the experience of being witnessed for who we are, not just what we do. Compassion is taking a moment to ask in an objective way, "What happened here? What must someone have been believing in order to do what they did?" You never really know what you'll discover. There's more to us all than what we can see on the surface.

Do we truly "see" each other?

There's also the reality that most of the time people aren't seeing each other anyway - they're projecting onto one another. It's easy to project ideals and images onto someone else, and most of the time we are unaware that we're even doing it. We're not really seeing another person, but who we think they are or should

118

be. Can we truly be compassionate with someone when we're seeing them as we think they *should* be, which essentially means judging them? Are we witnessing their essence? Compassion toward others is not only love in action, but vital to true intimacy, self-realization, and inner peace.

Let's take a look at compassion for the self, because it's really important if you want to get deep enough to see things clearly. This is another nuance of radical honesty, which enables you to loosen the ego's grip by shining a light on the dark. For the purpose of self-realization, we need compassion for those things we've done that we may not want to face.

I see a similar journey with a lot of people. When you first begin practicing radical honesty, sometimes the "easiest" place to start is being real with what you've allowed others to do to you - ways that you've given your power away, said 'yes' when you've really meant 'no,' and how you've played the victim.

Then, you get to the other side of the coin which is what you've done to others, how you've taken their power, imposed on others, projected onto them - the stuff that has, in many cases, a much bigger sting to it. This is where compassion comes in. It's truly the only way to be able to approach this kind of discovery. Compassion is going to show you the cause behind the behavior so you can see not only who you are, but who you aren't.

The cause behind hurting others

I'll give you an example from my own self-realization journey. When the false ego I had became more and more clear to me, I went through a period of having to acknowledge the things I had done that I felt awful about. I didn't want to see them and when I did, I felt a lot of guilt, remorse, and shame. After these initial feelings passed, I was able to compassionately look at the behavior, and it was easy to see the cause behind it. It was never as simple as hurting someone just to hurt them. I was trying to overcompensate for a place I felt truly lacking, or I was acting out of fear.

I had one of these big ahas when I got into an argument with my roommate at that time. Bottom line was that I accused her of pushing me away and rejecting me. I then remember going outside and sitting down and reflecting on it - and I observed something that completely startled me. I became aware in that moment that it was completely the other way around. I was rejecting her and pushing her away. I honestly didn't even know. I thought about all the ways that I did this on a daily basis, and I was filled with shame because not only had I done hurtful things, but then actually accused her of doing those very things to me.

After the sting of shame wore off, I could see the cause, which was an idea that began in childhood that I was unwanted on the planet. Discovering this through compassionate curiosity led me to a HUGE piece of what my false ego was built on. As I kept unpacking it, eventually that belief dissolved. I could finally see the truth, as opposed to the misinterpretations I had internalized to form an "I'm not wanted" belief as a child.

Compassion led me to finally be free of something that had kept me in enormous pain for my entire life. This was also the only way for the behavior to finally dissolve as well. When the root

120

cause dissolves, all the behavior caused from it does as well. Pretty freakin' cool how that works.

Seeing the light in others through our own darkness

Another lovely effect from turning compassion inward and seeing that doing "bad" things doesn't make you a "bad" person, is how it causes you to look at others. It's impossible to carry the same kind of surface criticisms of others when you've seen the light through your own darkness. Surface criticisms are painful for everyone. They cause anxiety for the critic as well as the person being criticized. As someone who used to walk around the world criticizing and rejecting everything, I can tell you that it's a terrible feeling not to see the good in anything or anyone. I'm now able to have a ton of compassion for others, because I always know there's more to the story then what I'm seeing on the surface. I also know that the *real truth is often only found underneath that surface.*

There's this idea that "your actions define you" which has been part of the mainstream for a long time. The concept is often misunderstood and isn't necessarily true for anyone. If we look at actions as defining whether we are simply "good" or "bad," then we're totally staying on the surface level which, as we're learning, is mostly false.

Yes, actions *can* be very revealing. They not only show who you are, but much more - what you're trying to be, what your beliefs are, how your imprinting has shaped you, what your genius is, what your interests and talents are. That's a lot of layers of knowing someone! So, you see how easy, and false, it can be to

121

make a snap judgment about yourself or someone else that is not accurate at all. Often snap judgements reveal a lot more about the judger than they do about the judged anyway.

Compassion holds space for our essence to emerge

Compassion also holds an open space to not only recognize true from false, but to feel and express any stuck emotions, which is really vital to the waking up process. Compassion says, "Let's see, let's feel, let's understand what's underneath the surface at the essence." It's a force that is all-loving, and welcomes all that exists. Compassion fears nothing, because it's open to everything. In most cases, we fear only what we don't understand, and when compassion is the focus, there is so much more to understand, so much more truth to see, and so much more freedom to feel.

It's a part of any awakening process to release and detox stuck emotions and stress. Compassion is more than just an intellectual observation, although it can begin that way. Have you ever had the experience of seeing another person, and witnessing that underneath the surface they're in a lot of pain? It can be a look in their eyes. Their face is smiling but their eyes say pain. Without saying anything, just your having witnessed the pain can cause an immediate expression of emotion for that person.

Maybe you've experienced this yourself. Have you ever tried to "keep it together" when something painful has happened? You lost someone you love, you had something hard happen, or you received some devastating news? You're sitting with a friend

122

thinking that you're pulling off the "I'm ok!" kind of thing, only to have your friend look at you in a way that lets you know they can see what's going on. And in that moment, like a dam breaking, you just let all your emotion out. It's happened to nearly everyone on some occasion. Your friend looked at you with compassion, they could see what you were trying to do on the surface but their gaze went right through your facade. And it felt like a relief.

Compassion is what's in play here - openly, honestly, and lovingly seeing the essence of a person. When you're turning compassion on yourself, you not only acknowledge what's going on underneath the image you're trying to uphold, but the "why." This may look like recognizing that underneath your confident exterior, you feel scared or insecure. That's where it starts. Then, you follow that thread and learn more about where that feeling came from. What's the belief that's holding it up? What happened to form that belief? Was it really yours, or someone else's?

And the most important questions: Is it real? Is it true? Is this even mine?

Instead of recognizing that you're insecure and just trying to be more confident (which rarely works for long), you dig down to the root and *that's* what gets examined. You don't focus just on the actions or behavior, you look at the *cause*. When you look close enough and question it, eventually you find that the belief loses its power, and you become free of it. Then the behavior changes on its own.

The closer you look at the foundation of the false ego and the emotional wounds that have caused its creation, the more it falls apart. Only beliefs and perceptions that remain unexamined and unquestioned can stay in place. The key is doing this with self-compassion, a great help in uncovering the truth and liberating you for good.

Compassion is a powerful force that can change lives. Imagine what we could do as a society that focused more on the essence than the behavior? Would we be so quick to punish, and more inclined to actually rehabilitate? Would we have much stronger and intimate connections with each other? Would we be so quick to criticize, or would we want to know more about the situation before we pass a snap judgment? Would fewer people feel misunderstood, invisible, or broken?

The answer is an emphatic HELL yes. Compassion can change your life for sure. As you begin to practice compassion, you'll feel different about what you see around you, and you'll find it much easier to love.

14 The Transformation Spiral

As you move through your self-realization journey, it's important to understand what I call "the transformation spiral" because it can help you move through the journey with a lot more peace. I observed this in my own journey and I'm grateful that I did, otherwise I may have been unaware of the progress I was making. It's also a wonderful thing that I'm able to pass onto my clients to help them see their own growth and development with much more clarity.

In the chapter "the little big things" I talked about focusing on and noticing the things that are changing. In this chapter, I'll share with you a bit about the things that *don't* seem to be changing, the "issues" that you seem to be coming up against again and again. There's a reason why certain things need to be revisited a few times, and it doesn't mean that you're not making progress. It means that you may be flowing down the transformation spiral.

Bumping into our issues … again and again

You're in the transformation spiral when you keep coming up against the same issue, but every time you do you see it from a slightly different angle or perspective. So, whenever the core wound, belief, or imprint rears its head, you see something new, feel something deeper, or have different insights and ahas about it. Depending on the depth of the issue and how close it is to the core foundation your false ego is built on, each one of those new angles reveals more and more to you. Each time you bump up against one of those angles, you are closer and closer to the dissolving of the issue for good.

Allow me to give you a real life example. In my own journey, I kept bumping up against the belief I mentioned earlier - that I was unwanted. I "knew" it intellectually, and could describe the issue and the effect to someone pretty well. That's where it began, simply identifying the foundation of which I had made an entire identity. When I first saw it, I was like, "Oh, THAT'S what the issue is!" and it was a very cathartic moment - a HUGE breakthrough that explained a *lot*. I could see what this belief had caused me to do, kept me from not doing, and how it dominated my entire life experience. It was a relief to see it. It was as if I had been followed by a mysterious shadow my whole life, and finally I could see what the shadow actually was.

It was SO monumental that I couldn't help thinking that I had solved a big problem in identifying it. I thought that once I saw it, the issue would disappear. That *is* what happened, but it didn't sure happen overnight (in the 24-hour sense). The seeing of it *began* that day. Once I put my finger on it I couldn't unsee it. I was no longer totally on autopilot and unaware. However, what happened after was not something I expected.

Once I became aware of the core issue, I would slide between observing it and participating in it. I would see it again and again. At first I saw it in my business. It became clear to me that a lot of the choices I was making, places I was gravitating toward, and goals I was setting were rooted in desperately trying to feel wanted, seen, and valuable. Each week that went by I saw it clearer and clearer. The more I saw, the more I felt empowered to do things differently, be more "myself," and I started feeling a lot less attached to certain things I depended on for validation. Woo hoo! Nailed that issue! Well, not quite yet.

Then I started seeing the "I'm unwanted" belief come up in relationships with my friends. I saw how much it was driving not only who I was choosing to be friends with, but also the dynamic of those relationships. For instance, sometimes I chose to be friends with popular or successful people just because standing next to them made me feel important - which meant that I was unconsciously using them. Sometimes I would lay guilt on people if they didn't spend enough time with me. Other times, I would find ways to reject anyone who got too close and push them away so I could validate that I was indeed...completely unwanted.

There were some big whopper ahas in my relationships with men - and a lot had stemmed from my relationship with my father. Feeling as if I wasn't wanted by my father was a big one for me. Most of my relationships with men were based on what I could give them or what I could do for them. When I was younger, I went to bed with anyone who gave me a tiny bit of attention. I felt so unlovable that I would pine for approval and bend over backwards to get it. Then, if I would get approval, the oddest thing would happen - I often would start searching for something that was wrong with them. I legitimately felt that if someone did want me, they must be messed-up in some way. It wasn't that I was picking the "wrong" men, it was the my unwanted belief was driving me to turn them into the wrong men in my mind. I had this "pine for you then reject you" OR I would push them away until they rejected me.

"Unwanted" also showed up in my relationship with life itself. On one hand, I felt like I had something to do on this planet. On the other hand, I felt like it would never be received and no one would ever want what I had to give. It was a completely hopeless feeling. This was driving my nearly constant thought of suicide. I felt like life didn't want me, and that made living in the world feel utterly impossible. Even though I hadn't had an actual suicide attempt since my 20's, the thought was there, lingering in the back of my mind right until the moment that my false ego dissolved.

Just as I am writing this, I realize that the thought of suicide isn't there anymore. I honestly hadn't noticed until this moment. I never imagined that I would be free of it.

Truth becomes more real than the lie

There's more to my story, as there always is. However, each one of these different angles revealed something. I knew, after examining this belief from all of these different angles, that it wasn't true. I didn't just know it intellectually. I KNEW it - and know it now.

Here's the bottom line: When I kept looking, the truth became more real than the lie. Each one of these steps was vital to the false ego having no more power, no more legs to stand on. I looked and looked, felt and felt, and didn't avoid anything. The false ego ONLY remains in place when it's left unexamined. Upon seeing it from this close up - it only has one choice: to dissolve.

The question often comes up: "But, why? Why do we get into the transformation spiral? Why do you need to see your core issue from so many different angles?" I actually don't know why anything is the way I've experienced it. My best guess is that we do this so we have nothing more to hang on to. It seems to be that the spiral is there to help fully cleanse us, by bringing us around and around again so we can see the entire truth by seeing the entire lie.

I can tell you this: that you're complete, that you need nothing from outside of yourself to validate who you are. I can tell you that living your life from your true nature is easier than pushing against it. I can tell you that none of the crap your inner critic is saying is true. I can tell you all of that, and on some level you may even believe it. The transformation spiral is when you go from simply *believing* to *experiencing*. That's where it leads.

Now you know. If you're not "done" with it yet, no worries. Each step brings you closer. Each time you hit the issue again you're doing so with more wisdom than you had before. That very wisdom reveals yet another and another lie that you've built your life on. And each time you recognize the lie, the truth begins to emerge. Stay the course, get help, and commit to the truth. The truth WILL set you free – again and again.

15 The Law of Attraction

I thought it would be fun to take some time in this book to dive into some of the common LOA teachings that, if they're not properly understood, may keep you stuck in cycles and patterns for years. In some cases there are some practices that can actually *keep* you from waking up, fully self-realizing and finally experiencing who you are without the "not enoughness" that's at the foundation of your false ego.

The purpose of this chapter is not to make anything "wrong," but simply to look at things a little more closely. There's value in every one of these teachings, if they're properly understood and questioned. If you question them, you can be in the unique position of taking pieces from what you're learning, and leaving others that don't make sense to *you* upon examination. It's even the same with the teachings from this very book. All of this should be run through your experience because your journey will be a one-of-a-kind path that is just yours. When you take the time to examine all teachings, you have the power to create your own recipe that works for you. You would be wise to take no one's teachings (including mine) at 100%. As Carl Sandburg said: "Beware of advice - even this."

Use the teachings of others to awaken yourself

What you're always getting from any teacher is *their* experience. It's a wonderful thing to share one's experience because it is valuable to others. When students are encouraged to question what they're learning, then you decide what works for you. When it comes to transformation - that's the whole point. Using the teachings of others to awaken yourself.

I'm sharing with you some ways that *I've* questioned teachings and what I've discovered as a result, so keep this in mind as you read on. Pay attention to what resonates with you - that is your guidance system at work. Most of what I've said over and over, from different angles in this book, is to look straight at your "stuff" instead of avoiding it, for the purpose of being able to consciously differentiate truth from lies. I tend to be the most critical of teachings that I feel, on some level, are encouraging avoidance.

Different methods of examination are as unique as the observer. Some teachings aren't actually teaching avoidance, but they can easily be misunderstood, and that's part of what we're going to look at here, so you can get the most out of what you're drawn to. Let's get started, and you can see what holds up for you, and what doesn't.

I'd like to begin with a topic that's brought a lot of personal growth into the mainstream, which is the Law of Attraction. The LOA is so often misunderstood; even that it is a universal law has caused some debate. Most of the teachings I'm going into here have some root in the LOA, so allow me to explain what I saw as I put the LOA under the Anastasia microscope.

Think about it and manifest it? Sign me up!

When I first heard about it, I thought it sounded fantastic. You mean, you think about stuff enough and you get it? Money, cars, even a soulmate? WA-HOO! Sign me UP for some of that! I was a very good student too. I did my affirmations, my visualizations, I talked about my manifestations as if they'd already happened, I focused on feeling good all the time - all of it. Of course every time something would show up that matched something I had been affirming, I was like, "OMG - I totally manifested that!" but when it didn't, I went into "I did something wrong" and immediately into "fix it" mode. I worked on "removing my blocks" to manifestation. I tried to change my beliefs, uplevel my mindset, clear, release, and clear some more. I would acknowledge the "good" as my aligned manifestation, and the "bad" would bring a feeling that I had something broken inside of me.

This kind of cycle went on for a while. I found myself in a lot of groups that talked about attraction and manifestation, so this conversation was very normal in my world. We were all having some version of "Yay! I manifested!" or "Boo! something bad showed up - time to clear a block!" going on. That made this type of cycle even harder to get out of. I wasn't questioning it, and neither was anyone else in my community.

When I did start questioning the teachings, I did so not to make them wrong, but to just question if I *really knew* what I was talking about. Maybe there's more to this? Does what I'm being taught line up with my experience? I mean - has it worked? Am I feeling better? Am I manifesting a lot of cool shit? Am I successful at clearing out my blocks, busting through my resistance, letting go of destructive patterns, feeling more peace, and living a life of my dreams? Is there always going to be this much effort? Is it ever going to get easier? Am I seeing this clearly, or is it possible that I've got this all wrong?

Can you create any damn thing you want?

The first thing I began to notice when I looked closely was that the focus on "fixing what was wrong so you can attract stuff" didn't hold water. I began to see that I was attracting what I wanted, *really wanted*, all the time, and it was very revealing. I started to see that approaching the self as if it's broken was never going to get anyone anywhere. I was so excited by this realization that I actually launched a business around it. I created an edgy message around miracles and attraction, and "creating any damn thing you want."

At the time, I was still rooted in my own not-enoughness, and even though I believed it fully when I was teaching it, the more I taught, the closer I looked, and the more my own teaching seemed to fall apart. I knew I had to stop talking about "attraction" in that way. But it can be difficult to say, "Well, I don't know if I can keep believing this" because it's threatening to the public image and reputation of a spiritual teacher. However, it was torture to keep on teaching something I knew isn't really true. I couldn't do it. I had to eat crow (again!) or make myself sick by lying to people every day.

So I've been on both sides, student and teacher. Based on what I observed from these points of view, instead of going into what didn't seem to "work," I'll share what I found to be true (for me) instead. My purpose is to bring this teaching closer to your self-realization. Your awakening. Your liberation. To relate with the LOA in a way that is helpful to your freedom, instead of keeping you stuck in the prison zone.

Here's a list of what I've learned about the Law of Attraction then we'll go through each one and dive in a bit.

1) The LOA is a giant mirror, there to help me awaken.

2) When I see everything that's showing up as a gift, I see the gift in everything that's showing up. This doesn't mean I'm always excited and happy about this gift; it means it's here to ultimately help me with what I'm *actually* wanting.

3) What I attract is an accurate reflection 100% of the time.

4) If I was *trying* to manifest anything it was coming from a place of lack 100% of the time.

5) Trying to feel "good" *all the time* makes no sense and is completely contradictory to the reality of the human experience.

6) Trying to change myself *so I can attract something* only makes me feel miserable in the long run.

7) There's no pile of gold or millions of dollars waiting for me when I *finally* come into vibrational alignment.

8) I can't just decide to change my beliefs, my mindset, or my vibration. They change on their own in a way I'll never be able to understand. How it works? Total mystery.

9) In some cases, the very *practice* of doing an affirmation is *only* affirming that I don't believe what I'm saying.

10) The LOA, if used as a tool for seeing reality, is helpful to awakening. The LOA, if used as a tool to *get* something, keeps me in prison.

Now let's look deeper at each of these....

1) The Law of Attraction is a giant mirror, there to help me awaken.

This is the basic way that I define what the LOA actually is. It makes sense to me. If I feel that the purpose of life itself is to self-realize, to experience one's divinity while in a human body (which I do), then the LOA suddenly becomes my best friend. It's instant feedback on what's going on inside of me, so I can see it clearly. When I see clearly, I can become more aware, more conscious of myself. The more conscious I become, the more I experience the truth. Then, I create and express not from a place of needing to get because I feel that I'm lacking something, but because it's what comes naturally.

The LOA is not here to fill me up (because I feel empty) or make me happy (because I feel sad), but simply to reflect. I see how life itself had created this as a way to show me without any interference, judgment, or imposition of any kind. Life isn't telling me what I should do. Life is showing me in real time what I believe and what I perceive.

All that's required is for me to open my eyes and stop denying what is right in front of me. I just need to look - and all the answers are right there. So I listen, instead of talking. I pay attention, instead of focusing on affirming and intending and visualizing what I think I want or need. When I lean in and listen and observe, I see that a lot more opens up to me than talking ever did.

2) When I see everything that's showing up as a gift, I see the gift in everything that's showing up. This doesn't mean I'm always excited and happy about this gift, it means it's here to ultimately help me with what I'm *actually* wanting.

I know now that everything, and I do mean everything, that was showing up in my life was helping me with what I actually wanted. You can probably look through your life experience and see the truth in this. I thought I wanted money, but money wasn't actually what I wanted. It was what I *thought* money would give me. This was true with everything I was wanting to create. It wasn't the "thing," it was the peace, fulfillment, and joy I imagined I would gain as a result.

It was only after I got all the stuff - the money, the house, all that shit - that I realized I was wrong. It not only didn't give me peace, but it caused more anxiety. I was more attached. I had more to lose. Accumulating "stuff" on a foundation of "not enough" produced more stress because I still didn't feel like "enough."

This hit me like a ton of bricks! It was the glorious LOA, like a patient friend in the corner of the room, that held the mirror up, saying, "Hmmmm, does that thought match the reality?" The answer was usually no. I began to get that I was focusing on what I believed would provide me what I wanted, instead of intending what I *really* wanted.

And it was only after I lost my money, my "status," a lot of friends, even my home - let it all go - that I realized I was actually in the process of manifesting what I really wanted: TO WAKE UP. To have the peace, the fulfillment, the joy, that comes from within and radiates outward. To feel this regardless of circumstance. Only then would I feel comfortable building anything. It must be built on a foundation of wholeness for me to enjoy any experience or circumstance fully.

I never would have asked for the experience I went through. But life heard me, and knew this was part of my journey. Lo and behold - life was right. When my intention was set to awakening, life took me on the exact right journey. Life is always taking care of you, even if it may seem like stuff is not working out. You may be getting something even greater than you've imagined.

3) What I attract is an accurate reflection 100% of the time.

I realized that by doubting this, I could stay in denial and miss the opportunity staring me in the face. To believe that what's showing up is *not* reflecting me accurately is having very little reverence for something that has far more intelligence than I can even fathom.

There's something quite mysterious, but most certainly benevolent that is always on my side. It's a force designed to show me who I really am. I realize that everything that's coming into my awareness has value. Most of all when I let go of the judgment of defining those things as "good" and "bad," this enables me to see past my own egoic preferences, concepts, and ideas into a deeper truth.

4) If I was *trying* to manifest anything it was coming from a place of lack 100% of the time.

This one surprised me when I saw it clearly. When I was operating from not-enoughness, the *wanting* itself was bubbling up from that place. I only then had an inkling of what I'm now experiencing. I became aware of this, especially watching a lot of awakened teachers - rarely, if ever, did they talk about manifesting money, situations, or circumstances.   In their awakened state they didn't "need" any of that stuff. It's not like they couldn't love and appreciate it, but they didn't need it to make themselves feel good. They could be in a state of enoughness living in a mansion or a shack.

I can see clearly that everything I was trying to manifest was ALL coming from lack. Every bit of it. Lack of worth, lack of trust, lack of peace - in all of those states these desires arose, and all of the desires were there because I felt they would fill the void.

On the other side of this, in an awakened state, the desire to manifest something isn't really there. I have an appreciation of the moment, a flow that feels good and natural. I know deep down that my life will always change, I have no need to try, just be and do from that being, and life will respond. I don't need to interfere in that.

When the false ego dissolves, the motivation shifts from "wanting" to expressing. It feels natural to do.

5) Trying to feel "good" *all the time* **makes no sense and is completely contradictory to the reality of the human experience.**

Geez, this is a big one. It's pretty self-explanatory, all I'll say is this: For me, peace and trust allow for *all of life* to be experienced. You can have ups and downs in your emotions and cycles. When you trust, you have no need to fight it at all. When I was *trying* to be cheery and positive all the time, well, the key word is "trying." In other words, I was pushing against what I was feeling.

I found that the deeper I went in my journey, the more uncomfortable feelings were coming up, and as I not only allowed them to be there but welcomed them, there was value there.

I remember on one occasion, I tapped into some deep inner rage. I stayed in my bed for nearly 24 hours straight and my body was actually twitching as some big stuff was bubbling up. This enabled me to clear out some repressed emotions that had clouded me for a long time. As it began to subside, I found huge insights about my childhood which led me to finally release some old beliefs that were simply not true, and what *was* true was there, clear as day. I couldn't hold on to those beliefs anymore.

I still find myself experiencing anger, irritation, sadness, and even grief from time to time. I don't resist, apologize for, or bury these feelings at all. I experience them in the moment, and then a very natural calm sets in. I have learned that those feelings are nothing to fear, just a part of life, and when they are experienced in the moment they pass quickly - and there are even greater levels of awakening on occasion. Sometimes things are just irritating!

I have come to understand that life comes with a rainbow of flavors: some bitter, some sweet, some sour, some savory - and they add a depth and richness to life's experiences.

Being "spiritual" doesn't mean pushing these things away. It's a way of seeing the big picture, the inherent value in all of life, fully allowing and experiencing everything. Suffering ONLY happens when this flow is resisted.

6) Trying to change myself *so I can attract something* only makes me feel miserable in the long run.

I've talked about my feelings of "not-enoughness." It was this feeling of lack that caused me to want to change myself to gain something. I felt that if I didn't have money, status, or the like that I would have no worth, and *that* was scary. It put a lot of pressure on the "stuff" to fulfill me, which of course it never did.

Once my focus went from *changing myself* so I could gain something, to *waking up* so I could feel fulfilled and whole and know who I really am - everything changed. I could see, feel, and experience real transformations, instead of the exhaustive chasing of something.

When I felt my not-enoughness (my false ego) melt, I didn't feel like I needed anything from outside of me anymore. Now I feel whole. The circumstances don't matter. I can enjoy nice things, comfortable surroundings, money, acknowledgment, appreciation, and kindness, but they are no longer coming from a feeling of lack. It's so liberating!

7) There's no pile of gold or millions of dollars waiting for me when I *finally* come into vibrational alignment.

When you actually do finally come into alignment, you don't need what you thought you needed. It's a wonderful feeling to know that you can have inner peace with nothing. It frees you up to have the life you truly are destined for. If you do have wealth and fame, it's because it's a natural expression of who you are.

The kinds of teachings that promised the gold at the end of the rainbow, at least for me, kept me in "fix-it" mode. They said that all I needed to do was focus harder on this, release that, and embrace the other - and then there was some big reward. In the future. I realized that this kind of teaching was the same as all teachings that promised that when I was "enough" in some way I would have access to riches and treasures.

I was fortunate to taste enough outer world success to know, 100% for sure, that it didn't change a damn thing inside of me. The jig was up! I could let go of the idea that millions of dollars would make me feel whole. The more aligned I actually was, the less the money mattered.

8) I can't just decide to change my beliefs, my mindset, or my vibration. They change on their own in a way I'll never be able to understand. How it works? Total mystery.

I chuckle a little bit when I hear, "These mindset shifts will bring (fill in the blank) to you. Just think (this way) instead of (this way)." Of course it's never actually that easy, but we're bombarded with messages that say it is. All I knew was that as I examined myself, my beliefs, and my perceptions, things began to just...change and shift.

Here's what I discovered: In order to change a mindset shift, the first thing is to realize that the way I am seeing the world isn't necessarily based on truth, that it could be questioned. When I say to myself things like, "Maybe I've got this all wrong. Maybe there's a different perception that's more aligned with who I am," not always right in that moment, but eventually, something else will just...occur to me. Sometimes very subtle, sometimes like a ton of bricks. Then, one day, I see things differently. I still don't know exactly how it happens - it just does. And it's the right answer.

The focus is from trying to control the change to being willing to be wrong and to open up to something new. It not only is easier to do, but is much more effective in the long run.

I watch this with my clients as well. Our focus is on self-discovery AND examination for the purpose of dissolving the not-enoughness. I watch them experience the same thing. They do it enough to notice that they are beginning to think differently, respond differently, and feel more confidence without "trying" (there's that word again!) to change. It's a glorious thing to witness.

9) In some cases, the very *practice* of doing an affirmation is *only* affirming that I don't believe what I'm saying.

I began noticing this early on. I didn't ever have to affirm things I actually believed - I just believed them. Every time I purposely affirmed "I have money!" "I am successful!" or something like that, it was rooted in a fear that I didn't believe it, and that I needed to believe it.

I have found that tweaking this was a bit more helpful. Instead of saying, "I have money!" I can turn it into a question like, "What do I really want that money will give me?" I often find that this brings up the real thing I want. Perhaps it's security. Maybe freedom. Even just some additional comforts. Then I can use those answers to probe deeper, with questions like, "OK, so I really want security. What IS that, actually?" This brings a lot of insights that lead me to truth. With most everything, I found that security or freedom, when I *really* looked at it, points me to a state of being, not an external circumstance. This quickly puts the focus there, instead of believing that money or success will give it to me.

There's of course nothing wrong in any way with money or success. But to look deeper and ask what you really feel it will give you can lead you to what you actually want.

The same is true for health issues, affirming "I am healthy!" to cure illnesses. From my observation, most illness comes from some form of fear or resistance. However, in some cases, the illness itself is manifested to give you something you're actually wanting. For instance, if you're feeling too obligated to others, or feeling stuck in a life that's not a good fit for you, illness can be a way out of that situation. This goes for physical or mental illness.

I often suffered from bad depressions - until I realized that depression was created in response to too much people-pleasing. When I was depressed I had the great gift of not having to take care of anyone, resting, and going into a cocoon that felt safe. I had a *reason,* because I couldn't just come out and say, "I don't want to" or "I don't feel like it" or a lovely, simple, "No, thank you." I needed depression to give me an excuse.

There's the story of an amazing, world-famous cellist who ended up with multiple sclerosis. Yes, she was one of the best cellists in the world, but, as the story unfolds, she in truth hated playing the cello. She was stuck playing this instrument that she didn't like - over and over.

It occurs to me that her MS could very well have been her only way "out." She couldn't tell the world that she didn't want to play anymore, but in a way, an illness that destroyed her ability to play could have been subconsciously manifested to help her get out. In this case, affirming health would have been useless. Coming out and saying "no" would have been difficult, but...would she have gotten sick? Who knows? It's just something to think about when illness comes. Could it be happening in response to something that you're wanting? Perhaps. Only by taking a look at your situation could you know for sure.

10) The LOA, if used as a tool for seeing reality, is helpful to awakening. The LOA, if used as a tool to try to *get* something, keeps me in prison.

The LOA is a wonderful, accurate mirror designed to show you all of those things that you feel are hiding. I remember saying, "How should I know what my subconscious beliefs are?" Well, they were all over the place, right in front of my eyes!

That's the beauty of this. If you see what's in front of you, you can really self-realize. If you stay in denial of what you see, you stay asleep. It's true.

The LOA, personal development, personal improvement, and self-help teachings can enrich your life for sure. They can offer new perspectives, insights, and realizations that are incredibly

146

valuable to an awakening journey. If these teachings are used to help you truly see, then you can begin to free yourself, and live the life that is most aligned with your nature.

What do you need - truly?

I invite you now to question what you think you need. Question what you think will fulfill you, make you whole, and give you peace. The illusion is that all these things are outside of you. Now is a good time to reflect on this in your life. Surely you've dreamed of something and gotten it. Maybe you dreamed that when you got a particular house, car, job, income, or partner that you would feel better. Maybe you thought that if you were attractive enough, got enough attention or validation, that you would finally feel good about yourself.

My questions to you now: Is that really true? Did it work? Did that external thing give you what you really wanted, which is to have peace? To trust the flow of life?

It's easy to sell someone their dream in "5 easy steps." All our false egos are forever in search of something on the outside to fill us up on the inside. Right now, I invite you to wake up to the truth. To see the Law of Attraction for what it really is: a mirror to help you awaken. In this moment, if you stop trying to use the Law of Attraction to get you "stuff" and begin seeing it for what it is, you'll be led down a path that will lead to greater fulfillment than anything that is external could ever deliver.

16 Tools for the Journey

In this chapter, we'll look at some tools to help you with your self-realization and awakening. However, I'd like to begin talking about tools by gently reminding you that, once again, it's truly up to you to pay attention to what resonates. This is where talk of tools and practices can get a bit tricky, because people are all designed very differently. I noticed this a lot during my own journey, and see it with my clients as well. We forget that what "works" for one person may not "work" for another.

The way I usually suggest practices is through paying attention to who my client is, and since I can't do that here, I'll just remind you that these are simply tools to help you get to *your* truth. You will always have your own individual process, and no tool or practice is magic in itself.

The practice is there to point you to something valuable and create space for that awareness to happen. The practice itself really isn't the point, the recognition of truth *is*.

There *are* practices that you do for the sake of the practice, simply because it makes you feel good, such as physical exercise. Some people love the gym. Some love a walk, or to dance or swim. The point of the practice is to move your body because the body works better when it gets some movement! The point of exercise is not *always* about getting somewhere: skinnier, bigger muscles, etc.

Exercise can be one of those things that is practiced with NO goal in mind, simply doing it for the enjoyment of it. Unfortunately, exercise has been, for a long time, a thing you do to become more desirable or acceptable, so it's become a burden, an obstacle; the "work" you need to do if you want to get a "result." The truth is, exercise just helps your body, brain - pretty much everything - function better. In an awakening journey, getting out and getting a bit of movement can help tremendously.

I heard a popular spiritual teacher once say, "If people would just eat a pretty good diet, get a little exercise, and enough sleep, most of their problems would disappear." That's really quite true. I call this "baseline care," these things that keep you well-functioning, so that you can handle the self-realization process even better. However, I know it's easier said than done, especially if what your false ego believes is keeping you from taking care of yourself (like you should be over-giving and over-doing for others), which we've talked about a lot in this book.

Try what's right for the true you

There's also something else to consider when we talk of practices and tools for self-realization and awakening. Remember, people are different. For example, certain people are like the tortoise and some are like the hare. I know some people who are solid and grounded in their nature, and some who are like the busy buzzing bees. Now, for the buzzing bee types, a 2-

hour meditation may *not* be the best way for them to access their truth. For them it may be journaling or talking. For the more solid, slower moving types, sitting in that long meditation may be the absolute *best* way to have their life-changing insights. Should the hare try to adapt to the slow-moving tortoise way, or the tortoise try to keep up with the hare? Nope. You must find out for yourself, and *trying* things is the key.

Keep this in mind when you hear teachings that announce, "this is the way." I invite you to add a "...for them" at the end of the sentence, and then ask yourself, "What value can I take from this? How can I use this teaching to create an awareness in me?" These specific questions can enable you to take value out of every teaching, even if it's simply pointing you to something that doesn't have anything to do with the teaching itself.

For example, if you hear something like, "If you want to awaken you must meditate for 5 hours a day" and you ask the questions above, then you can: 1. Try a few 5-hour meditations and see what it's like; 2. Instantly know that's not how you work, and use it to point you toward a better way for you to create space for awareness; 3. Take a different meditation route; or 4. Feel a resonance instantly and discover that 5-hour meditations are indeed *your* thing.

In this way, *all teachings* can help with some big self-realization, discovering who you are, and also revealing who you are *not*. Use the suggestions in this chapter as you see fit and just dismiss anything that you don't like. I'll share some of my personal favorites as well as some things that I've witnessed others gaining huge ahas from. So let's dive in.

Q&A Journaling

My personal favorite way of waking up, I'm sure you're not going to be surprised at all, is questioning things. I know I've said this a lot, but I'll now get into some specifics so you know a bit more of *how* to question in an effective way.

Let's start with what's <u>not at ALL</u> effective, because it's so commonly done and is very unproductive. It's easy to ask questions that don't really produce any truth, but can keep you swirling in lies and fantasy. I'm sure you've experienced "swirling" at some point in your life. Questions like:

"Why do I do this?"
"What's wrong with me?"
"Why do I keep hurting myself?"
"Why can't I get unstuck?"
"Why am I so fucked up?"

Questions like this can easily keep you in a cycle that doesn't get you anywhere. You don't have to take my word for it, try it and see. Chances are you have asked or been asked questions like this, so you probably know this well.

Ask questions for which you *want* the answers.

You can ask questions many ways, but I highly recommend Q&A Journaling. This is journaling with a specific purpose, and writing can be a lot clearer than just thinking, because thoughts can jump all over the place. Plus, you can see it on paper which can be helpful!

I encourage you to approach this inquiry as a way to become more conscious, aware, and awake, by shining a light on what has not been seen before. Inquiry is a way to get to know who you are, and who you are not. It's a way of taking something in life that you're having an "issue" with and using it as a jumping-off point to look deeper, *not* as a way to get something. If that's why you're doing the inquiry it will cloud what you're able to see.

It can begin with a simple intention to have no agenda other than discovery. See what you see. Think of this exercise as opening the door to a dark basement - a place you've inadvertently thrown a lot of stuff that's cluttering up your space - and shining a flashlight on it. The way to "clean" the space IS by shining a flashlight on it. The closer you look, the more you see that the "junk" is almost like a hologram. It looks real but it's not. Inquiry enables you to truly see this, and *that's the point* of it.

A notebook, pen, and comfy chair are all that you need here. I suggest journaling for at least 20 minutes, more if you like. It can even be helpful to actually set a timer, as your false ego may want to find a way to wiggle out of this type of practice, because it can't survive under examination. It only stays in place when you're looking in another direction. A minimum of 20 minutes can reveal quite a bit.

The practice is simple: It begins with simply writing a question down, and then writing whatever answer comes up. I often tell

152

my clients, "I don't know" is not an optional answer! If you start with the guideline that you aren't allowed to write "I don't know," then *something* will come out. This type of practice can not only help discovery, but the dissolving of the false ego.

It's also important to say here that an inquiry like this is good to do more than once. You can ask different questions each time and see what the answers reveal. You have different awareness all the time, every day.

Example: The "money issue"

Let's take a specific situation as an example: Imagine that you're having trouble with money. Money stresses you out, but you can't seem to stop chasing it, worrying about it, dreaming of it, or feeling that it will solve all your problems. You want to look deeper to see where an inquiry about money will take you, because you want to feel peace about it, ultimately.

Q&A Journaling is a different way to approach a "money issue." In the personal development world, I've seen a lot of approaches to money come from trying to just create a whole new reality, which is fine, but the problem is that the desire to create a new money reality is rooted somewhere in feeling that you need money to feel peace. So most of the whole approach to the money issue will be coming from a deep feeling of lack which, as you now know, will not get you to the root of the issue or bring you what you truly want.

Money is a useful example because it's something that affects nearly everyone, and most of us have a huge charge around it.

That charge can lead you to some *huge* awakenings which will free you from the stress you feel around money, and ultimately that's what you want. Most money stress is bubbling up from somewhere else, and when the focus is on money it's a way of putting your attention on the symptom, or in some cases the distraction, from the *real* issue.

You can use some of the suggested questions I'm about to share, or you can ask questions in response to the answers you get. There's really no right or wrong way, just ask questions and something fascinating will be revealed to you.

You can easily replace the word "money" here with body, weight, relationship, career, family, or many other so-called "problems" we all face. Approach all of these as simply a way in, a door that invites you to know who you truly are, and all you need to do is to walk through.

Here are some questions to get you started:

- What is my money situation reflecting for me?

- Where did I get my beliefs about money? Are they even mine? What do those beliefs reveal about me?

- What triggers me about money, or people who have it (or don't have it)? What do those triggers reveal about me?

- What is this money issue trying to show me? How is it here to help me awaken?

- What does money represent for me?

All of these questions will lead to answers which will lead to more questions. Follow them, and you'll discover something that's previously been hiding from you. Remember, the false ego cannot keep its foothold when questioned and scrutinized. Pay attention to where your intuition guides you. Sometimes the awarenesses you have will point you to something else that is necessary to awaken. Questioning the things that often get taken for granted as truth will reveal something valuable, and in some cases, life-changing. Just this simple practice can cause many old patterns and beliefs to dissolve over time.

Example: "Trigger, projection, imprinting issues"

Q&A Journaling is a great tool for deep, insightful self-reflection. This can take a lot of courage to do, but remember, the sting of seeing something you're hiding passes quickly, and what you're left with is a feeling of liberation.

You can use Q&A Journaling to dive deeper into projections, triggers, and especially childhood imprinting and all the beliefs and perceptions you formed during that time.

It's a moment to sit and get very real with yourself, and examine what you've been buying into your whole life.

Let's say you're feeling triggered by something or someone. The first step is to take full responsibility for your trigger, blaming no one else for your reaction. The object is to get curious about what exactly is being triggered inside of you. Most of us are triggered when we're feeling as if we're not enough, unworthy, wrong, or unlovable in some way. It's easy to get defensive in those situations and when you do, it's important to look at what you're defending and why.

So sit and ask questions like these questions:

- What am I defending here?

- Why do I feel the need to defend it?

- What am I afraid to see?

- Why am I afraid to see it?

- Is my point of view the only correct one?

- What if it's not?

- What's behind someone else's point of view?

- How do I feel when someone tells me I'm wrong?

- Do I connect my inherent worth to being right?

- If so, how do I do that?

- How am I affecting others when I do that?

- What do I want others to see?

- Why do I want them to see that?

- Am I seeing what they want me to see, or am I more concerned with being seen?

- What do my judgments reveal about me?

- What are the beliefs behind my judgments?

- What am I projecting onto others?

- What do I need to see here to finally release this trigger?

Take a moment and imagine the impact of this type of inquiry. What would happen if we, collectively, stopped defending, projecting, and bickering long enough to ask ourselves these questions? How much intimacy and connection could we have then?

Take courage - Dive deep!

It takes, as I've said before, enormous courage to go there. However, when you do, that's the way to take off the veil of illusion and see what's really going on. Then you can deal with it more effectively. What you hide from yourself and others is what controls you. What you look at doesn't control you - it's that simple.

Looking at things square in the face is what consciousness is all about. It's not about pretending to be something you're not, feel something you don't, or behave some way that will bring approval from someone else who's probably got their own issues anyway. Consciousness is not about wearing certain clothes or fitting into a certain mold.

Consciousness is hard in the beginning, because there is a mountain of stuff that you're hiding from yourself for a good reason. The more you see, the more liberation you'll feel. Don't take my word for it - try it for yourself and you'll see.

The Observer Intention

This is a great tool that you can use often, and goes very well with the Q&A Journaling. Consciously going into the "observer perspective" is a key piece of the disillusion of the false ego. The observer perspective begins with a simple intention: to observe yourself objectively for the purposes of waking up.

I'll give you an example from my own life. I had a huge realization a few years ago about how my belief that I was unwanted caused me to create this circumstance again and again. The belief came from many things, but a lot of it came from my relationship with my father.

My father really wasn't that into being a dad. He did what was common in the 60's and 70's, which was to get married young and start a family, because he felt like he was supposed to. It's not that he didn't love me, and he certainly did the best he could. But the truth is, he actually was bothered by my presence. I get it, kids can be amazing *and* very annoying at times! Phrases like "children should be seen and not heard" exist for a reason.

I was quite the handful: hyperactive as well as sickly. I was pretty much bouncing off the walls from day one. My parents told me that one night I crawled out of my crib 13 times - 13 times during the night they would have to get up and try to get me back to sleep! This happened a lot. I always wanted attention and it was hard for any adult to have a moment's peace when I was around. I actually *was* kind of a pain in the butt.

My dad didn't want to do daddy/daughter outings with me. He didn't get excited about hearing how my day was, or have things he wanted to teach me. He didn't love spending time with me. The only time he did like spending time with me was when we were watching TV, basically, when I was quiet.

It wasn't *just* my dad. I was basically born into a family that didn't really know how to deal with a spunky, slightly special needs child. For the first 10 years of my life, nearly every room I was in had *someone* in there feeling annoyed with me. This is how I got the vibe that "no one wants me around" which became the foundation on which I built my false ego. I spent my life believing it. I not only created the scenario over and over, but also would interpret events to validate that was true. It was a very lonely existence for a long, long time.

When I first began to see this clearly, I would consciously go into situations *intending to observe*, so there was always a background awareness just *watching* the situation. The more I observed, the more I could see all the interesting ways I overcompensated for believing that I'm unwanted. I saw clearly how I was usually pining for love, attention, or validation OR pushing someone away. What was interesting about this observation is that the more I did, the more I realized that it's not true that I'm unwanted. I slowly but surely saw the situation more and more clearly. When my false ego finally dissolved, I was able to look back on my childhood and see it for what it was. It wasn't personal, it wasn't that I was unwanted or unlovable. It was that I was simply a handful, and the parents who did love me just didn't quite know how to handle it. That's it. There's no more charge or feeling "wounded." I've seen clearly that the "wound" was from seeing the situation from a particular perspective. Once the perspective changes, there's no more wound. Between questioning and observing, the unwanted thing couldn't hold any more water.

How the Observer Intention works

The observer intention is quite simple: Before you walk into a situation, intend to observe yourself. This takes you out of being solely on autopilot and allows you to have an enormous amount of self-awareness. The more you can see, the more choice you have. The more freedom you have.

Questioning and observing really require a lot of radical honesty (remember the power of radical honesty we talked about in Chapter 8?). Have you ever been in a situation where you behaved in a way you're not proud of, and at the time blamed someone else for it? Then, a few days later you got this flash of clarity, and you have that "oh shit" sting of realization - that someone else was actually not to blame, but you were just triggered?

Even though that stuff is not always fun to see, every time you do see it, you can't keep repeating the behavior again. Only when you refuse to see do you not only keep repeating it over and over, but you stay in that tight little slightly hellish prison where most everything in your life is a way of overcompensating for some way that you feel broken.

This can look like trouble in relationships, career, or health. It can be the morning look in the mirror in which the reflection never seems to be good enough. It can be that feeling of disappointment that comes from not getting a lot of likes on Facebook, or not feeling validated from people around you. It can be those things you think but you can't say. It can feel like you're needing something you don't have pretty much all the time.

All of these things are NOT part of the "human condition." They are not an inevitable part of life. They *only* exist when you're operating from not-enoughness or feeling broken in some way. With enough questioning and observing, you WILL see the truth. The truth is awesome. The truth is, of course you're wanted, of course you're (more than) good enough, of course you belong here. Imagine living from that place. Yes, it feels much better!

Mindfulness

Mindfulness is another wonderful tool that is a space creator. Mindfulness is a practice that *helps with being able to observe*, because it trains your thoughts to slow down a bit.

I'm not the best mindfulness teacher out there. There are a lot of books, programs, and resources that are great at giving you all kinds of ways to bring more mindfulness into your daily life. There are even some great smartphone apps that can help with a mindfulness practice.

Mindfulness is defined as:

1) The quality or state of being conscious or aware of something.

2) A mental state achieved by focusing one's awareness on the present moment, while calmly acknowledging and accepting one's feelings, thoughts, and bodily sensations, used as a therapeutic technique.

Mindful eating - 100% attention

A classic mindfulness exercise is about eating. Most of us are doing something else while we're eating: talking, watching TV, playing with our smartphone. Mindful eating is a very cool thing to try.

Imagine doing this: Put the food on your fork, bring it up to your eyes and look very closely at it. Then, smell it with a deep inhale. Then, open your mouth, bring the mouthful in, and really pay attention to the taste, texture, and temperature. Notice all the different flavors, allowing it to stay in your mouth to enjoy it fully before swallowing.

It's all about putting 100% of your attention on the meal. Even if you don't do this at every meal, it's a really fun way to eat. I remember purposely going to a restaurant once for a mindful meal. I even let the waiter choose everything: from my wine, to the appetizer, entree, and dessert. Eating that meal took me 90 delicious minutes (*I normally shovel the food in my mouth as if someone is going to take it from me!*) and I still can remember some of the tastes and smells. I remember everything I ate. I remember the scenery, the restaurant, even how the waiter looked. It turned eating into a sensory explosion - just by doing nothing more than paying attention to it.

Mindfulness can also be as easy as taking a deep breath or 2 for 10 or 15 seconds, and fully putting your attention on how the breath feels, how your body feels, and what's happening around you.

Mindfulness, as with all these tools I'm sharing with you, is not a "do it once" or "do it for a week" and be done with it. TV, internet, smartphones, and other tech are changing our brains to be a lot more prone to distraction, which keeps us asleep and unaware. All of these practices help your focus, calm, and presence, which will make an enormous difference in your awakening.

Vulnerability as a practice

Let's start talking about vulnerability with a big truth: *Only the false ego feels a need to hide and protect itself.* Vulnerability is a conscious practice that you can start today, and the more you open yourself up, the less of a grip your false ego will have on you.

Vulnerability is usually defined as opening yourself to be hurt in some way. The type of vulnerability I'm speaking of here is more of an emotional vulnerability. I'm not suggesting that you walk down a crime-filled street with a shirt that says "easy target." That would go against your natural survival instinct anyway. This is about opening yourself up so that you are expressing yourself freely and authentically and allowing others to see you in a deeper way. If you ever want to experience any real connection and intimacy, total and complete vulnerability will take you there.

The peaceful warrior - absolute vulnerability

In self-realization and awakening, vulnerability plays a big part in shining the light on what was once dark, hidden, and repressed. Remember, you hid it away or repressed it for a good reason, even if it was unconscious. You shoved down anything that would threaten the image you created to gain approval from others. You shoved down anything that you believed made you bad, wrong, unlovable, unworthy, or not good enough.

Practicing opening yourself is a way to, step by step, look those fears right in the face. Each time you do they begin to release their grip. With each fear that begins to dissolve, you feel freer, bolder, and stronger. There's a great quote in Dan Millman's book, *Way of the Peaceful Warrior*:

"The peaceful warrior's way is not about invulnerability, but absolute vulnerability."

Vulnerability is the ultimate act of trust. It seeks not to protect, but to open. It's a "bring it on" kind of approach to life, in which the world can be fully embraced as it is. If you want freedom, it requires vulnerability. You are not free as long as you feel that you need a wall between yourself and the world. An awakened life, a person who sees reality for what it is, someone who trusts, is open.

With that said, vulnerability is nearly impossible to the false ego, so you need to start where you are. Baby steps are fine. It's difficult (and unnecessary) to go from being very closed to very open, and depending on who you are it can feel traumatic to do so. Taking small steps leads to bigger ones, and over time you can walk through the world feeling safe, supported, and open to whatever life brings.

The fear of feeling

Vulnerability starts with acknowledging your feelings. Oftentimes it's easy to repress feelings because we have been brought up with the idea that certain feelings are not OK to feel - things like sadness, anger, even frustration. When you repress anything, you repress everything. Repression is repression. If you can't feel fully angry, you can't experience fully joyful. If you can't feel fully sad, you can't feel fully happy. Often we don't feel safe to experience emotions fully for a variety of reasons. If you grew up with a parent who was violent, you may believe that feeling any kind of anger is wrong. The truth is, violence and rage come from repressed sadness or anger. The more you repress, the worse it is. Every human feels these feelings and there's nothing to be afraid of.

165

The fear of the feeling is what makes things go very wrong, not the feeling itself. When experienced fully, emotions are fluid and pass a lot quicker than if you're trying to *not* feel it - which is the irony here, isn't it? Acknowledging emotions, especially if you're used to repressing them, can feel very scary at first. It can be a much easier process if you call on some loving support. However, sometimes friends or family have their own issues with feeling their feelings, and it can be difficult for them to support you in those moments. Often people want to move past it quickly, cheer you up, or change the subject. So in many cases, the guidance of a professional can really make it easier and feel safer. A good coach or therapist who knows the value of feeling emotions can hold a great space for you.

Vulnerable communication - witness to your truth

Vulnerability can also be practiced through communication with others. Speaking your truth is a powerful practice of letting something out that you are hiding, as well as letting someone in to witness you. I have a great friend who is good with this. I've had moments where I've said some things out loud that are painful to say and feel shameful to reveal. She's responded with just listening, and saying, "I witness you." She doesn't give me suggestions or advice, she just lets me know that I'm safe to express these things. I've had huge personal breakthroughs in those conversations.

It is important to note something here about "speaking your truth" because it can easily be misinterpreted. Sometimes people, under the guise of speaking their truth, can blame, belittle, or guilt another person. Speaking your truth is not, "You did something wrong and I'm hurt by it." Speaking your truth is, "I feel triggered." It's not asking someone else to change to keep from triggering you. For example, saying something like "When you do this, I get triggered, so can you stop doing it?" is not speaking your truth. It's blame. Vulnerable communication is not asking another person to alter their behavior. It's revealing something that you're hiding, and allowing them to witness you.

Sometimes vulnerable communication is simply talking about something that has nothing to do with the person you're talking with, but just opening up to them. It's a wonderful thing to preface vulnerable communication with what you actually *do* want from them. For example, *"I want to open myself up and tell you something. I just need a witness. You don't have to give me any advice, or even say anything in response. It's super helpful just to listen. Would you be willing to do that for me?"* This lets someone know their role so they can relax, lean in and be there for you. Any trusted friend or family member will appreciate the opportunity to do this for you.

The reason why we're so scared of vulnerable communication is that the false ego fears being judged or rejected by others. What usually happens when you open up is that someone else feels much safer to also open up. And the reality is that some people will get turned off by vulnerability. It's important to remember that has nothing to do with you. As we explored in the chapter on triggers, what you judge or reject is only revealing your stuff. Your beliefs. Your concepts of right and wrong, good and bad.

It's good to remember that if you are rejected by another person for being open and vulnerable, it's probably a good thing, because this is a person that may prefer your false ego to the real you. They're not bad for being that way, it's simply reflective of their own stuff. It also doesn't mean they must be eliminated from your life, they could simply go from being a close friend to someone you go to the movies with every now and again, which is totally fine. It's up to you, and I trust that you can feel the situation out for yourself and decide what's best.

Vulnerability is a practice that opens enormous learning, opportunities to discover, and the disillusion of your false ego. The bottom line here: Whatever you feel you need to hide has enormous power over you and keeps you stuck, because you have to work so hard to uphold your image. It's incredibly liberating to disempower the image, the "false you" that doesn't actually exist. You only are letting go of what you're *trying* to be. The you that you actually are is much better, much more authentic, and much *easier* to be. Because it's the only thing that's real.

Releasing Attachments

If you're like a hot air balloon, attachments are like the sandbags weighing you down. Attachments are often confused with love, which they are *not*.

Attachments are 100% fear-based.

Anything that you feel you can't let go of comes from the idea that without it, you will be incomplete. The truth is that

168

everything is fluid, impermanent, and ever-changing. In reality we hold on to nothing. We continue to change throughout our lives. People come and go, circumstances come and go, even our physical bodies won't last forever. You can love, appreciate, and value much more deeply when you're not attached to it.

A process I do with my clients in the beginning of our coaching is centered on releasing attachments to outward approval, which sometimes are attachments to the false ego itself. When attachments are released, you can flow with life so much more easily. Attachments are like weights tied to your ankles and backpacks full of rocks. They're heavy and they slow you down.

Going through life unattached does *not* mean being an island, a lone wolf, or never owning any property, nice things, or having people you love in your life. Not at all. You can be in a long-term relationship without being attached. You can have a job or career that you love without being attached to it. You can have a beautiful home and a nice car and a comfy bed without being attached to it. You can have a thriving community of friends and loved ones without being attached to them.

Also, being unattached does not mean that if you lose something you don't feel any sense of grief. You can be unattached to your loved ones, and when they pass away you will miss them very much. You can enjoy your home, and if you move away you may still have a sense of sadness about saying goodbye. You will even feel, on occasion, some grief for the loss of your false ego, just because you lived with it for so long.

Attachment actually cuts you off

Going through life attached to anything, refusing to let things, situations, or people go is painful because it cuts you off from reality. It's that simple: *When you push against reality it's painful.* Attachments in romantic relationships, the idea that without this person your joy or life will end, puts you in a position of insecurity. It also places a ridiculous amount of pressure on the other person to be your sole ray of sunshine, and as you probably know by now, that doesn't last. Because nothing lasts. Everything is in a constant state of flux, evolving faster than you can even imagine. Even life as we know it changes. We live in a different world than we did 100 years ago or 10,000 years ago.

The good news is that you are built - you are hard-wired - whether you know it or not, to go with the flow of life. Humans have an incredible, amazing ability to adapt - and adapt quickly. The false ego fears change, which is another way of saying it fears reality, and lies to you when it tells you that you need to hang on to something because you need it. It feels better to go with the flow because it's the natural order of things. It doesn't mean that you don't feel an array of feelings when something changes. This is why being afraid of painful feelings can keep you attached. Yes, if you enjoy something or you're simply used to something, the separation has, depending on how deep it is, a painful feeling associated with it. It does pass, especially when you accept that there's no way around this. This is part of life. It's nothing to fear.

I often say, "If you don't cry when you leave a situation, you didn't fully enjoy it."

I've been through this many times in my life. Even though I've wanted to move and leave things behind in my life, and felt totally aligned with it, I still experienced grief. It's the birth/death cycle I wrote about earlier. I've learned to honor the pain of any death or change and feel it fully, only because I've seen the truth: Hanging onto something that's naturally ready to change, evolve, or die is 100X MORE painful. The pain of a natural separation passes much more quickly than the pain of trying hard to keep everything the same.

Releasing attachments ritual

Releasing attachments can start with just this awareness. It can start with something as simple as cleaning out a closet, and letting go of that which you're not using, no longer need, or doesn't reflect who you really are. If you've ever had the experience of literally cleaning something out like a closet, a garage, a drawer or cabinet, thrown things away and created some more space, do you remember feeling it in your body? It feels like a deep breath, a relief, a calm that washes over you. There's a reason for that! We feel good when we let things go that no longer are a reflection of us. We go into a new situation and adapt quickly. And the cycle of letting go, adapting to the new, experiencing life, and letting go again continues.

Self-realization and awakening are all about letting things go. It's impossible to experience who you truly are if you're not willing to let go of who you aren't. Consciously and mindfully releasing attachments are key.

Releasing attachments is a wonderful thing to do in a ritual. If you're aware that you are attached to something, *meaning that you feel <u>you'll be incomplete</u> in some way without it,* you can do this little ceremony which will bring a lot of awareness and awakening to you.

1) Bring to mind the attachment. It could be your car, house, romantic partner, a belief, circumstance, children, or approval from others. You probably have more attachments than you think, so start with what occurs to you first.

2) Close your eyes and bring to mind everything you feel about the fear of letting go, or why you're attached to that thing. The awareness of "I'm afraid of who I'll be without this" is plenty. As you have this thought, pay close attention to the feelings in your body. Tune in deeply. Oftentimes you'll feel anxiety, sadness, even anger or frustration. Just bring all of your attention to those feelings. Scan your body, and send the intention that any feelings associated with this attachment make themselves known. Stay with it a few minutes. Just be with those feelings.

3) Declare out loud: *"I totally release the attachment to _____ "*. Then, either through the top of your head or the bottom of your feet, visualize all of those feelings

going up into the sky or down into the earth. It may help to give them a color or texture as you do this.

4) Declare out loud: *"I accept that I am whole and in the flow of life. I accept the space for the new. I am open."* If you like, visualize a cleansing light coming down from the sky and permeating through every nook and cranny of your body and energy.

5) Take a few deep breaths. You'll probably feel relaxed and relieved. Repeat this as much as you want, and feel free to repeat it with the same thing until you feel a sense of relief, or choose another attachment.

When you release attachment to anything, you can be yourself with it. You can be open, vulnerable, and authentic. You can truly love. You can enjoy it fully. You can appreciate all of life in a way that is deeper and richer. Try it and see for yourself.

New Things, Small Steps

Releasing attachments, being open and vulnerable, questioning and observing all lead to an open approach to life. A really effective awakening practice is to "shake it up" on a regular basis. This is a very conscious tool that you can use to open yourself up in little, or even big, ways to something new.

New things give us opportunities. We get to see things from different sides. We get to come out of our routine and find new ways to learn things about ourselves. I find that new things can not only reveal core genius, but challenge that which we believe to be true.

Variety, the spice of life

Trying new things is not always about trying to change everything all of the time. Certain routines we have can be grounding, and there's certainly nothing wrong with some things in your life that are familiar. You can enjoy the familiar without being attached to it. Trying new things is about being aware of having things *too* familiar and <u>consciously</u> bringing variety into your life. It could start with going to a different grocery store than you usually go to. Making a slight change in your morning routine from time to time. Going for a hike in a new location. Trying a new restaurant on occasion. Changing up your breakfast, lunch or dinner every now and again, and cooking a new recipe. Rearranging your furniture here and there, or redecorating in some fun ways every couple of years. Even changing out the pictures you have in frames for new ones. Trying a new coffee drink. Doing a different workout or exercise class. In those little things, you may find a new opportunity, something you like or don't like, or a new awareness or discovery that may change everything for you.

Of course there's travel and adventure which also can be fun. Even taking an overnight trip to somewhere pretty, going to visit an old friend, or finally planning that month-long trip to Europe. You can go zip lining, horseback riding, or sign up for a salsa or belly dancing class. Go have a spa day at different places, or even test drive a fancy car - just for the purpose of seeing yourself in different situations, and taking a moment to observe what those new situations bring up for you.

It doesn't matter really what you choose, but do think of this as a divine spiritual practice. A way to learn and explore not only new things, but *yourself* in new situations and circumstances. This is a practice that teaches you how adaptable you truly are. One of the biggest benefits to this type of practice is this:

You become less afraid of the unknown, and much more open to the flow of life.

This can be fun to do with someone else as well. A "shake it up" buddy that you get together with to try new things is a lovely way to experience a friendship. Even if it's someone you talk to about the little things, such as sending a "here's how I shook it up today" text message, like *"Usually I wake up and brush my teeth and then floss. Today I flossed first instead!"* That kind of thing can be fun to share.

Even if you do this on your own, keeping track of the things can be a great way for you to reflect. A "shake it up" daily journal can accomplish this. Not everything needs to be huge or scary. It's simply about keeping you aware and conscious, and even little things like this are quite useful to help you wake up from autopilot, bring more mindfulness into your life, and stay in the flow.

Embracing Reality

I couldn't talk about tools for self-realization and awakening and skip over this one! Embracing reality IS a practice for acknowledging what *is*. It's the practice of looking things in the face instead of avoiding them.

I've covered this in bits and pieces, but I'd like to go deeper into it here. The biggest lie of the false ego is that fantasy is *preferable* to reality. The lie is that fantasy is full of bright colors and endless possibilities, and reality is boring, gray, and full of obligations and responsibilities.

Let's be absolutely clear...

Reality is that...

You are a genius at being YOU.

You are capable of change, growth, and expansion.

You have infinite possibilities available to you.

Life is about expression and experience, and it's easier when you're in the flow.

You actually *can* handle things.

You are more supported than you realize, and you are not alone.

You are very much supposed to be here.

You are not only "good enough" but you are perfect in every way.

You have enormous power inside of you.

Embracing reality looks like mindful planning and organization. Managing your money and your resources. Taking care of your body because it makes you feel better when you do.

Embracing reality is realizing that self-awareness, responsibility, and good communication actually make things easier. Looking at what's there and acknowledging it. Accepting what is.

Embracing reality is taking care of things that need to be taken care of; preferring to escape reality and live in fantasy means that things pile up in the corner, things go undone, unsaid, and unrealized. Embracing reality sometimes looks like admitting to yourself that you haven't dealt with things, but that you can.

Embracing reality is waking up to the truth that suppressing hurts a *lot worse* than expressing, because it's totally unnatural to do so.

Embracing reality is realizing that life is full of many experiences, emotions, birth and death, ups and downs. It's saying YES, I *know* that nothing is permanent.

Embracing reality is letting go of attachments, and creating space in your life.

Embracing reality is realizing that you can't do everything on your own. That you need support sometimes, and that you have to ask for it when you do.

Embracing reality is enjoying this beautiful life as it is, and going *with* it instead of pushing against it.

Embracing reality is to open your eyes and consider that there's more to you, more to life, more to the world, and more to the universe than you can see, touch, taste, smell, or feel. There IS an energy, a mystery, something that always will remain unexplained. There's always something to explore and learn.

Embracing reality is realizing that you will accomplish more with a beginner's mind than with thinking that you'll ever be remotely close to knowing it all. You never will. EVER.

Embracing reality is to see that people are different and unique. Not everyone works the same way, that your way is your way, and theirs is just as valid. Those differences are necessary for a functioning ecosystem.

Embracing reality is to know that there are infinite paths to the same destination.

Embracing reality is to awaken. In fact, that's *all* awakening is. It's taking off the veil and seeing things how they really are. Seeing yourself as you really are.

Embrace reality. It's much more peaceful.

Celebration

Speaking of embracing reality…

Celebration is a huge part of transformation. Often we forget to celebrate the little things. In the chapter "the little big things" I talked about this, but I'd like to offer this to you as a real practice, a great tool for transformation that can lead to many openings in your life.

In many personal development circles, a gratitude practice is common. It is indeed a great practice, to feel grateful and appreciative. I feel that celebration is just as important. Celebration is a way to step into the observer role for a minute and notice yourself. When you're looking for something to celebrate, it naturally leads into a self-awareness and reflection space.

What you focus on expands

We have talked about self-realization and awakening from many angles. There are also some great tools you can use for the journey. When you take time to celebrate what you realized, did, noticed, became aware of, released, changed, expressed, or opened, you are actually activating the practice of "what you focus on, expands."

I feel like celebration is a good practice to do at the end of the day, because it's reflective to look back on the day and celebrate *something*. You may celebrate that you acknowledged your feelings today. You may celebrate that you became aware of something you've repressed. You may celebrate that you spoke up, shook it up, or even that you accomplished something that feels good.

You can keep a celebration journal, or share with a friend. I often have clients text me with celebrations they want to share because

I absolutely love to hear about them! It's a joy to celebrate with someone, but it's just as amazing to take the moment for yourself if you prefer.

Meditation

Meditation, in some way, shape, or form, is pretty vital to self-realization. Meditation is a way to listen, create space, focus inward, practice presence, reflect, or even just relax. There are many ways to meditate, depending on who you are. As we talked about in Chapter 16 (Tools for the journey), you may be the kind of person who loves to sit in a 5-hour meditation and drift off to other dimensions. You may be a buzzy bee who is well-suited for a brief 15-minute meditation.

Inner stillness

Basically, meditation is stillness. In the middle of everything it's necessary to find some kind of stillness to do the discovery/dissolving process of awakening. Mostly, meditation is done by sitting still. However, you can access stillness in movement, even though it seems like a contradiction in terms. The stillness I'm referring to is inner stillness, and there are many ways to tap in. Some people do a yoga practice. Some do walking meditations. Some people meditate through some type of creative activity, such as making art. Meditation and stillness can be found in a variety of ways.

The first time I asked someone "how do I meditate?" the answer I got was: "Just sit there and don't do anything for 15 or 20 minutes." It seemed nearly impossible at the time. Now I find it so interesting that simply sitting for a period of time without doing anything (watching tv, playing with the phone, computer, etc.) is so difficult. I remember thinking at the time that sitting still would make me feel crazy. I was instructed to just "watch my thoughts" even though I had no idea what that even meant. Now I explain it like this: "When you decide to sit there and not do anything, you may even expect that your mind is going to go nuts. Sit there anyway."

In some cases, it can be helpful to use an "anchor," something that brings you back from your crazy mind for a few seconds. You can use a mantra, which is just a word or a phrase that you repeat over and over. It gives your mind something to do. You can just think this mantra to yourself, or some people say it out loud as a repetitive chant. Another great anchor is breath awareness, which is just witnessing your breath. When you meditate, every time you remember, just come back to breath awareness or your mantra. And, again - expect that you will drift into your thoughts. If you go in knowing that's probably going to happen then you'll be less likely to get mad at it!

A lot of people go into meditation thinking that their mind is going to shut down and be totally clear. That may or may not happen depending on your individual nature. If it does happen it usually comes after lots of practice and patience. But you must realize that you can soak up the benefits of meditation without a totally clear mind and no thoughts, so try not to make "getting there" the *point* of it. It's not. The point of it is to be still for a while. Just use an anchor, set a timer, turn on some nice music if you like, and breathe. You'll discover what meditation can do for you once you try it for a little while.

181

Be still in a world of noise and distraction

Meditation is really super-duper necessary in today's world because of so many distractions that we're subject to, which absolutely keep people on autopilot. There's no space carved out in many societies for personal reflection and stillness. In fact, these things are often seen as luxuries in some sense, as something that's unnessary to survival, success, or thriving in the world. Of course that's totally backwards, as most of our society is!

When I lived in Northern California, I frequently used to go to this place called Harbin Hot Springs. It was always amazing what I experienced there. They had no cell phone signal there, no TV in the rooms, no phone, and the internet they did have was old and crappy (for a reason!) - it was a total technology detox. I would go and stay for a week. The first 24 hours took some getting used to. I was aware, only then, how much I was reaching for my phone during the day. It was hard to stop and settle down. By day 5, I could sit in a chair for 3 hours doing nothing. Not reading, journaling...just doing nothing. I could just sit there and *be*. In those moments it became clear to me that 500 years ago it was probably easier to meditate! But humans are amazingly adaptable and learn quickly. Taking a daily space to turn things off and just BE is incredibly healing, as well as a vital practice for getting off autopilot, and exploring your truth.

Summing Up...

There are many tools that can help you reveal what's true, let go of what's not true, and live a truly aligned life. None of these tools in itself is the magic pill, that's not what tools are. That's not what practices are. The purpose of them is to help you to see, to know, who you are. Pay attention to that.

Be aware that, in some cases, the tool or practice itself can become a crutch, an addition, or an attachment. It's like being on a journey to a beautiful mountaintop and becoming attached to one of the signposts so you never get to the peak. It's just a signpost pointing the way, not the destination. As you explore these tools, keep your eye on the reason for them: Revealing and experiencing truth. Truth is the mountaintop that's ever-reaching higher heights of existence. If truth is your ultimate commitment, you *will* find it.

17 Conclusion and Next Steps

In this book you and I have taken quite the journey together. We've explored the ego, self-realization, love, waking up, and some tools for the journey. You've heard exactly what you needed to hear. You've responded to this in a way that is perfect for where you are, right now. If you pick up this book in a year, you may get totally new insights and realizations. If you share this book with a friend you may see someone who has a very different interpretation, and one that is just as valid. All is perfect. You'll find that to be 100% true, 100% of the time.

There's an old saying: "When the student is ready the teacher appears." It works that way because when you're ready for something, you begin *looking*. You tune your spiritual antenna to a different frequency, and you hear and see all new things. Maybe they were even there the whole time, circling just outside of your peripheral vision, patiently waiting there until you turned your head slightly further - and there, seemingly like magic, the perfect message, teacher, or opportunity is right there, reminding you that life is indeed taking excellent care of you.

You are loved no matter what

Life doesn't impose. There is nothing "up there" with a sense of right and wrong judging what you do. That's a human thing that can only happen when the perception is very narrow. A divine perspective - and just imagine it for a moment - sees all possibilities, forms of life, and expressions. Everything IS divine. There is nothing that isn't. Only the divine is real. Remember this. Take it in for a moment.

Life, the universe, God, *whatever you call that force that is bigger than you,* has NO agenda. None. You are loved no matter what. You can do the most heroic thing, or the most horrific, and it's all the same to the divine. The divine has a perspective that is so enormous, it's impossible to insult it. Only a false ego gets insulted, offended, or angry because you didn't comply with its ideas of right and wrong.

This is often great to know - and scary to know. It's the ultimate realization that your life has no outside agenda. You're being shown and guided based on who you are and what you want. God only wants for you what you want for you. You have no need to gain approval with your actions, thoughts, or feelings. You are actually, totally, and completely UNCONDITIONALLY LOVED. What would it truly do for your life is you realized this?

The only reason for this insight to be scary is this: All most of us have ever known is the endless search for approval from outside of ourselves. We regulate our behavior by it. We motivate our lives by it. In some ways, it can be a "comforting" structure to live our life by. Don't steal, don't kill, don't lie, etc. - most of us understand those rules. If we had nothing judging us, how would we regulate ourselves? Would our motivation dry up? Would the world just become chaos if our collective God suddenly had no requirements of us to get into heaven?

Well, of course the answer is an *emphatic* "no." If we look at the reality, the "rules" haven't stopped war, violence, or disease. The rules, generally speaking, haven't made us feel more peace. Living our life based on outside rules is a concept most of us are very attached to, but if we look closely, it ceases to hold water. The reality is totally different than the theory. If we never question anything and just keep buying into certain ideas, the cycle will continue - until it finally reaches a critical point. The bubble bursts. Then, we need to find a new way.

We're at one of those critical times right now

The bubble IS bursting. On a mass level a bubble bursting can be something that takes hundreds or a few thousand years, which is just a "speck" of time on a bigger scale. Humans have been on a path that is following a particular evolutionary purpose. We first learn to stay alive. Then we go through the stages to do more than survive, but to experience our potential.

Right now, we're moving out of competition and into connection. I know it may seem like it's happening slowly, but it's not. It's happening incredibly fast in the grand scheme of things.

First we realize our connection to each other. Then, to the environment and all the ecosystems in it. Then, finally, our connection to the force that binds it all together. This is where we reach a particular way to function that is harmonious and productive. It is a way of life that is coming, but I believe still a few hundred or thousand years away. We're still learning right now, and the seeming chaos of the world is a huge part of WHY this evolution is going to take place. We collectively need to learn what works and what doesn't. All that's required to evolve is to, on some level, get on the same page with each other. What's happening now is eventually going to lead to this.

In this moment, YOU are a key part of this evolution. You are like a single cell in the body. You are waking up to something. You are questioning what you know. You are open to new possibilities. You are seeking. Your eyes are opening, your heart is opening. Like a single cell, a seemingly small lifeform, you - without even trying - are having an impact on the cells around you. Then, there becomes a group, the group then has a bigger impact, and so on until the entire body becomes transformed.

This doesn't happen overnight in the 24-hour sense. But, taking a bird's eye view, a few thousand years is very much an overnight change. The best thing you can do right now is to keep waking up. Keep realizing who you are. Make decisions that are in alignment with the truths you continue to uncover. Be courageous and willing to let go of what you're holding on to that you KNOW is false. Say how you feel. Let the chips fall where they may. Open yourself up more and more each day. Your awakening will not only create more peace for you, but will naturally radiate outward.

Core Genius Coaching and the Self-Realization Collective

It's important to have a guide on your awakening journey. I couldn't do this alone. No one really can, because at some point a curious witness can not only help you see past your own blind spots, but open you up to new possibilities.

It's my life path to be this curious witness. I love it more than I can ever express. To be invited into someone's world is an honor. To see their genius is a thrill - and to point it out and watch them embody it is pure ecstasy for me. This is my way of expressing, creating a more awakened world that works. It's the thing my whole life has led toward, the reason I've always been able to see underneath the surface. I first had to turn this on myself, and now I'm taking others on their own path to freedom.

If you feel drawn, I invite you to experience Core Genius Coaching for yourself. It's a profound journey of being witnessed for who you are. And you walk away with a "Core Genius Map" that can help you navigate your life with more awareness, truth, and peace. It's a very healing experience. A Core Genius Map reveals your particular life purpose and the core genius you were born with, which helps you not only understand who you are, but navigate through your life with much greater ease. You stop pushing against your nature, and go with it, because you know what it IS.

Core genius can not only be a part of career and business transitions - but how to know the right relationship/s for you, what particular type of self-care practices are more likely to be a good fit, why some things are easy and some are challenging. It will reveal what you need to consider with every major life decision. If each of the Core Genius Elements are ticked off the list - you will be fulfilled and expressed no matter what you do. It's like an insurance policy for your life.

After we discover the Core Genius, we look to integrate the new discoveries into your life. I personally hold your hand through the application of what you discover, who you are, and the process of continuing letting go of that which is not aligned with your true self.

Along with the Core Genius Map, I offer a Core Values Map. Values can be defined by what you believe is important. For instance, my top value is truth. Under that, communication, vulnerability, openness, freedom, and personal expression are for sure what I think are the most important things in life. When you know, and can name your values, this not only impacts the REASON for your purpose but how you relate with the world around you. Knowing your values is a vital piece of to relating with others, as well as life itself.

When you know your values this can open up an awareness that other people also value what they think is important, and when we have different values and can respect their differences we can share real intimacy, as well as learn a lot from each other. Knowing your values is not only a key to knowing the self - but it is truly the basis of ALL RELATIONSHIPS.

For example, let's say that you value, more than anything, spiritual development. When this is what you consider to be the most important thing in life, someone who values money and success may be perceived as shallow, or having the *wrong* values. Of course, they feel the same way about your values.

When you understand that what you value is part of your particular life journey, and another person's values are perfect for their life journey, then you can open up and realize that if you approach money and success as a legitimate value (which it is for them,) you may be able to have a peaceful and productive interaction with that person. This type of knowing can open you up in ways you can only imagine. This is a true "God's Eye" view. Seeing the beauty in the value in things simply because they exist. This is love in action.

Core Genius AND Core Values paint a very custom picture of your unique recipe. This is the discovery piece of self-realization that very few people get to experience at this depth, but as one does, life begins to make a lot more sense. You know your place in the world. To me, this is the real key to feeling that sense of belonging. You don't twist yourself into a pretzel to fit in. You stand in the uniqueness, seeing how you are one very important cog in the wheel, so to speak. You belong BECAUSE you offer this unique piece.

You feel that sense of oneness and peace because you can see that other unique pieces make up a big picture, one that works and functions well. You see your sameness AND your uniqueness at the same time, which is the most wonderful thing about being human.

You're also welcome to check out the Self-Realization Collective, which is a group of people who are exploring awakening and truth. In this group I go deeper into these teachings, answer your questions, and provide insights and resources for you to explore.

You can find all of this on my website at http://AnastasiaNetri.com. I also put up blog posts from time to time that you may enjoy.

You matter - your participation matters

You are at the precipice of a new consciousness that is exploding in the world right now. You are the center of it. Your participation in this matters. You matter. You are part of something that is greater and bigger than anything you can imagine, and you are vital to this evolution. Your life has purpose and meaning. You are a unique creation that offers a puzzle piece in the coming together of it all.

It's been my honor to share this with you, and I hope that our paths will continue to cross as we move forward on our awakening together.

Until then - stay the path. Remember, you're not alone. You are one of many brave souls who are being called into consciousness. You matter. You're loved. Most importantly: You have it all, right now. Everything you're seeking. It's all there, waiting to have the light shone on it.

If you're on an awakening path, you are indeed a Badass. Awakening is as Ninja as it gets. So, you're a Badass Ninja. Don't forget it.

Acknowledgments

I'd like to thank my Mom for being a model of true love, my biggest fan, my best friend, and by far the most spectacular support system that I've ever experienced.

I'd like to thank my Dad for his support, my Sister for her encouragement, and my Aunt for believing in me so much.

Thank you, Bettyanne Green, for your huge contribution to this book.

I'd also like to thank David for the vital role you played in my awakening.

I'd also like to thank Paula, Toni, Jacque, Renee, Stacie, Freda, Leslie, Christine, Sharon, Carol, and Jessamina for being such an important part of this discovery and for what each of you opened up to, and what each of you brought out of me.

Enjoyed what you just read? Please take a second to leave me a review on AMAZON.COM

About the Author

Anastasia Netri is a transformational coach who "doesn't sugarcoat spirituality and personal growth in fluffy New Age cliches." Her first published book, "Self Realization for Regular People" was birthed from her own awakening experience in which she lost her "false ego". Once she could see the truth, the words in this book exploded from her.

Her flagship product is the **Core Genius Map**, the foundation of her coaching services. She is also the founder of the Self-Realization Collective, a membership group with teachings, practices, tools, and community support. Grounded in her keen knack for business (starting her first successful company at the age of 22) and lifted by her own journey toward self-realization (starting in her 40s), Anastasia is gifted at seeing her clients through the darkest pain and the brightest light, holding safe space for them to go deep, and delivering measurable results in their personal and business lives.

To know more about Anastasia, visit her website at www.anastasianetri.com

Made in the USA
Columbia, SC
25 February 2020